THE TERRORISTS

THE
TERRORISTS

LAURAN PAINE

ROBERT HALE & COMPANY · LONDON

© *Lauran Paine 1975*
First published in Great Britain 1975

ISBN 0 7091 4977 8

Robert Hale & Company
Clerkenwell House
Clerkenwell Green
London EC1R 0HT

Composed by Specialised Offset Services Ltd, Liverpool
and printed in Great Britain by
Redwood Press Ltd, Trowbridge

CONTENTS

ILLUSTRATIONS

ONE

The Structure Of Terrorism

As far back as there has been a written history of man, violent efforts to change established systems of rule have existed. Overlordship in all its forms has invariably brought forth some kind of opposition. Since men submitted to the first chieftain or despot, and perhaps even earlier, there has been a division between those at the bottom and those at the top. Until the advent of Magna Carta, and later, adequate communications, the power at the top usually did not have much trouble coping with dissent from the bottom. After King John's capitulation in 1215 at Runnymede, dissent, often in league with liberty, proliferated and progressed. When liberty or some semblence of enfranchisement became common, at least in the Western World, dissent continued, its bases not wholly different from historic opposition. This was rooted in social and economic disparities, but the rights of humanity to assemble and to dissent, to exert initiative, have turned the forces of opposition in historic times into fully committed revolutionaries, which, in fact, most modern dissenters are – revolutionaries guaranteed the right of revolt by the indulgence of free societies which are themselves often the targets of the revolutionaries.

Today dissenters, like all other groups, are more numerous than at any time in history. They represent a greater disparity between ideologies, between classes, cultures and races than ever before in history. The technology of the strong, rich, and advanced, have put into the hands of modern dissenters, means by which dissent can at will, seriously or capriciously, shock the world.

This was demonstrated in Munich during the XX Olympiad when Arab terrorists killed eleven Israelis. It was demonstrated earlier, in May of 1972, when three Japanese terrorists opened fire at Lydda Airport in Tel Aviv killing almost thirty totally unsuspecting people. It has been demonstrated daily since the end of The Second World War, somewhere in the world, and it has confirmed two significant facts. One, that today dissent is powerfully funded, and two, that dissent is no longer only dissent; now it is terrorism.

Terrorism in the latter third of the twentieth century despite contrary allegations, is not a fresh phenomenon, a sudden alarming, recent innovation. The Middle East, Asia, Europe, America and Africa have all experienced terrorism subsequent to the Second World War, and in most of those places someone decried the emergence in enlightened times, of nihilists, anarchists or radical leftists — whatever term was being currently applied to terrorists — as though terrorism were a variety of dissent, so new in the world that as yet no one had devised a defence against it. But in fact, terrorism — although currently and almost universally considered as the exclusive prerogative of students, violent radicals and infiltrating leftists — has always been most successfully employed, not by bomb-hurling anarchists and political cretins of the left, but by governments and ruling hierarchies.

Within the realm of the recent past, beginning in the year 1792 and ending in 1794, during France's Reign of Terror, French terrorists known as Jacobins brought nation-wide disruption, violence and terror to an established state, presenting Europe, and . as much of the rest of the world as cared to look, with an excellent example of how terrorism worked, and how, under certain social conditions, it could succeed.

More recently, in the year 1921, Italian fascists, better organised, more nationalistic than their principal opponents, the Bolsheviks, successfully employed terrorisation, while the supine Italian monarchy abstained from interfering, and in October of 1921, Benito Mussolini, the fascist overlord, became Italy's Premier. Although he initially upheld the law and enjoined moderation among his *fascisti*, once he was thoroughly entrenched in power, all opposition to fascism was met with violence and terror. The story of this particular epoch of terror was both complicated and prolonged. In fact, Italian fascism endured for a longer period of time than any relatively recent reign of terror (excluding only one — Russian terror) beginning in 1921 and lasting until Italy's defeat in 1945 at the conclusion of the Second World War — a period of twenty-four years.

During this epoch terrorism in Italy was directed against all opponents of fascism, and employed all the traditional practices of terrorism, including assassination and beatings, torture and harrassment, intimidation, murder, and arson.

Still later, in Germany, commencing about 1931, terrorism as an instrument of compulsion and intimidation was successfully employed by the National Socialists — the Nazis — until, in 1933, Nazi leader Adolf Hitler became Chancellor of Germany, and subsequently Nazi terrorism, ultimately in league with fascist terrorism, was exported to Western Europe, Africa, and later to all of Europe, until the outbreak of warfare on an international scale was assured, and of course ensued.

Nazi terrorism was ended, in conjunction with the death of fascist terrorism, in 1945, and both events occurred almost simultaneously with the violent passing of the two men, Mussolini and Hitler, who had successfully created both.

Terrorism, then, was not altogether a nihilist nor a leftist option. In fact, in its most virulent and powerful forms it was rarely spontaneous and still more rarely nihilistic. True, it has most recently been equated with low-level activist protest, or with some kind of violent minority upheaval, and in this context it has become most commonplace and most recognisable. But actually the variety of police-state oppression currently practised in the U.S.S.R., successor to both the fascist and Nazi terrorist regimes, is by far the greater terrorism, even though we will not primarily concern ourselves with this kind of terrorism in the ensuing pages, but shall confine ourselves to terrorism in the former categories because it has been most spectacular as well as most commonplace and recognisable.

Nevertheless, terrorism by fiat, mandate, or free-choice is more powerful, difficult to dislodge or overcome, and is far more lethal when practised by established, and entrenched rule. Also, when terrorism becomes entrenched, it is usually rightist, or nationalistic, not leftist, while currently, at least, violent dissent at the lower levels is almost without exception leftist. Both Mussolini and Hitler achieved supremacy by overcoming leftist violence in their countries by opposing it with rightist terror. In America a few years back a presidential aspirant, Senator Barry Goldwater of Arizona, an ardent rightist, echoed the philosophy of the far right by adopting as his campaign slogan the aphorism that 'extremism in the defense of liberty is not wrong', and subsequently, although denunciation against this philosophy rang out across the land, a significant number of Americans, roughly 16 million, voted in support of Goldwater and his dictum, which implied that extremism, meaning terrorism, which has historically been the hand-maiden of any kind of extremism, was there, alive and well, and evidently thriving, although remaining in abeyance, in the United States.

However, even though we will not primarily concern ourselves here with entrenched terrorism, since many national treasuries actively, and even openly, fund terrorist groups, it would be impossible to divorce one from the other, and at least in this regard established governments are not only involved in terrorism, but in some instances control, or guide, or export terrorism.

For the past quarter-century communism has emerged pre-eminent in this field. Sir Winston Churchill prophetically noted the reason for this over forty years ago when he said. "Communism is not only a creed. It is a plan of campaign. A communist is not only the holder of certain opinions; he is the pledged adept of a well-thought-out means of enforcing them. The anatomy of discontent and revolution has been studied in every phase and aspect, and a veritable drill book prepared for subverting all existing institutions . . . No faith need be, indeed may be, kept with non-communists. Every act of goodwill, of tolerance, of conciliation . . . is to be utilized for . . ." the ruin of enemies of communism. "Then, when the time is ripe and the moment opportune, every form of violence from mob revolt to (terrorism) and private assassination must be used without stint or compunction . . . and once the apparatus of power is in the hands of the brotherhood, all opposition, all contrary opinions must be extinguished by death."

The strongest and most active terrorist organisations which have surfaced in the world since the end of the Second World War, have been communist oriented and communist financed. Every prominent terrorist group has accepted funds, weapons, or supervision from communist sources, even such outwardly self-serving groups as Ireland's fighting factions, and the ardently pro-Islam *Al Fatah* federation of Arab dissidents whose proclaimed purpose is the restoration to Arab countries of the lands lost to Israel during the Six Day War.

Thus it would be impossible to divorce terrorism from an 'Establishment'; some Establishment, somewhere. In Latin America terrorists have been financed and encouraged by the United States as well as by the U.S.S.R. In many cases Soviet aid and encouragement has been handled through revolutionary Communist Cuba, and on the right, the forces of opposition terrorism have received U.S. aid through a number of entrenched rightist, or nationalist governments, if not directly from the U.S. Central Intelligence Agency.

There was a time when bands of Robin Hood-like guerillas existed, not accomplishing much beyond harassment and aggravation, notably in places such as Mexico, China, the African territories, and even in the south-western United States, but technological advances in such detection devices as aerial surveillance pretty well obliterated them, and in any case those bands were never really dedicated to anything beyond plunder. In those days even Marxism as the forerunning of communism, was seldom the real reason that such bands existed, although a few well-read guerillas claimed this was the case.

Terrorism, however, as a kind of endemic malignancy, achieved its current sophistication right along with all other varieties of social alteration; as the times changed so did the theory and practice of terrorism until, in the Sixties and Seventies of the present century any terrorist belonging to a recognised group of terrorists was as well armed, financed and trained, as was any member of the Establishment opposition, such as the police, and in many instances he was better armed, trained, and financed. The day of the slovenly, carefree, Mexican *bandido* kind of terrorist was beyond recall.

China's factional 'Tongs' faded, as did the terrorist on horseback in
Islam, or the bedaubed head-hunting African. They were replaced
by the Mau Mau, the Red Guards, Islam's *Fedayeen*, Japan's *Rengo
Sekigun*, Mexico's disciplined communist party, or, on the right,
Mexico's tough, dead-shot nationalist-terrorist group, the *Halcones*
(Falcons), all deriving their sustaining life's blood from the treasury
of an entrenched Establishment somewhere — Moscow, Havana,
Peking, Washington, Paris, London, Berlin, Tokyo.

Fundamentally, they were all advocates of something people
could identify with and put their hopes in; some faith or ideology
which promised, not necessarily a sudden Nirvana, but at least a
life holding more promise than their current existence. Their
conviction was, for many, an amalgam of sectional partisanship,
extremist patriotism, and despair of anything better ever arriving
unless it was compelled to do so through gun-barrel diplomacy, also
known as terrorism. At their apogee, they were fanatics in whom the
failure of religion and politics to deliver anyone from despair had
driven to take matters into their own hands; they had as little faith
in their priests as in their politicians, something which in many
cases was entirely justified. A paradise after death was not a
practical advocacy to those deprived of their homes on earth, who
lived in constant pain from hunger, and in endless squalor and
sordidness. Anything at all was better than existing as fourth-rate
human beings — even death — providing that in achieving it, a
backlash of the lifelong resentment, misery and hatred, could injure
whatever it was the terrorist considered at fault for his degradation.

Politicians manipulated terrorists exactly as they did enfranchised
majorities, and were in turn assassinated by terrorists of the
opposition. Ideologies strengthened and gave purpose to those
driven to terrorism by despair and hatred, even though the
ideologies very often did not coincide with individual, regional, or
national opinion (which has traditionally been the posture of
communism — a system dedicated to the full use and exploitation of
dissenters) until triumph arrived. After that, those known to be
capable of fomenting dissatisfaction, particularly among
communists, were put to death.

Terrorism, then, emerged as a pattern of hopelessness. But this did not preclude its growth, nor its manipulation. It also emerged as the sump towards which misfits gravitated .by the hundreds of thousands. It became for the hopeless and psychotic, the militantly unstable and immature, as well as the persecuted (actual and imaginary) the homeless, hungry, and those of diminished capability, a refuge for grouping and for groping towards something which they could serve and believe in; something they could identify with.

It has been the classical plateau for the disenfranchised throughout history, but until recent times it had never been able to stun the world nor really alter the course of history very much. Not until it was able to make full use of modern technology — wireless, television, sophisticated weaponry, air travel, international funding — could regional terrorism make an impression and influence the politics and the policies of nations.

Now it can. For the past quarter century it has been progressing steadily towards that goal. The infamous assassination of eleven Israeli athletes at the XX Olympiad in Munich in early September of 1972 by Arab terrorists, was followed from start to finish by television cameras whose viewing audiences were world-wide. Hour by hour the tragedy was carried live, *via* the most modern mass-media reading and viewing techniques. Heads of state in at least a dozen countries became involved, millions of people were shocked into immobility before television sets in Europe, the Americas, Asia and even Africa, by an act of terrorism being carried out by exactly eight men. Terrorism had come of age. Finally, the misfits, the immature and unstable, as well as those with genuine grievances, all who had turned to terrorism for the redress they felt each was entitled to from established society, by forming into federations or groups and parties, were able to intimidate a million times their numbers, and do it so successfully that great and powerful nations were obliged to take heed.

Each terrorist success ensured prestige for all terrorists. It also appeared to ensure greater recognition and funding. In Vietnam those who were originally called simply 'Vietnamese Communists' 'Vietcong', an unflattering colloquialism, ultimately evolved into a terrorist organisation capable of compelling the strongest nation in the world, the United States of America, to not only recognise them as equals at a peace negotiation in 1973, but to acquiesce in great measure to their demands for ending the decade-old Vietnamese War.

The Vietcong were terrorists. They were financed, armed, trained, and largely supervised by the Communist Democratic Republic of Vietnam. They were additionally sustained by at least six red-bloc nations, as well as by contributions from a number of non red-bloc nations such as Sweden. Whether the position of the Vietcong was defensible or indefensible is not at issue here; what *is* at issue is the plain fact that the Vietcong began their active existence, not as soldiers, but as terrorists, arsonists, assassins, violent dissenters. But before they met the Americans at the peace-negotiations, they had convinced the world that terrorism could no longer be categorised as a kind of regional and isolated social aberration.

They waged a successful, endless war against France, the United States, and also against their own kind, the people of South Vietnam. With aid from allies to the north, as well as beyond Indo China, they succeeded. Finally, because the Vietcong, all terrorists in fact, including the eight *Fedayeen* who killed the Israelis at Munich, operated from a very simple concept, they possessed a great advantage. Their purpose was exclusively to kill, to destroy, demoralise and paralyse, while those who opposed them had, at the same time they attempted to overcome terrorists, to defend, protect and repair.

The success of terrorism could in great measure be attributed to the fact that very few nations (none in the West) and no national leader who is dependent upon a benign image for his political popularity and success, have moved against terrorists with anything approaching the equivalent relentlessness employed by terrorists against organised society.

There are other reasons for their successes, to be certain, but as Winston Churchill implied, the terrorist is a fanatic, and historically fanatacism has only been overcome by a greater determination, a greater fanaticism. It can be doubted that any such dedication and sacrifice will be found, in the future, among any people, including

Europeans and Americans, whose pursuit of pleasure and leisure is augmented and sustained by ample employment, high wages, and material prosperity unequalled in history, even when these people come face to face with the stark fact that the power, and the numbers, of the terrorists are increasing.

TWO

There Are No Boundaries

The common conviction among police and government authorities in Europe and the United States is that there is no such thing as an international terrorist conspiracy.

That may be true if by a 'conspiracy' is meant a centralised, unified, terrorist organisation, or what might be termed an international commission, or high-command, which issues orders and sends forth terrorist cadres, but it would be absurd to say there is no *rapport*, no sympathetic affinity among international terrorists. There is entirely too much hard evidence to the contrary. Also, since much of terrorism's leftism is Soviet oriented, unless one excludes this very definite world-wide apparatus, which is most certainly an international conspiracy supervised from within the Soviet Union, one can hardly accept as a fact the statement that terrorism is not in one regard an organised effort, and in another regard, a cooperative effort.

For example, British intelligence agents who were interested in how the Irish Republican Army managed to obtain rockets and launchers which had been manufactured in the Soviet Union, discovered that, subsequent to the U.S.S.R.'s rejection of Britain's request that the Soviets abstain from interference in troubled Ireland, the Irish Republican Army (I.R.A.) obtained its Russian weapons from Arab terrorists operating through arms supply depots in Switzerland.

The weapons had initially been furnished by the U.S.S.R. to Syria for use against the Israelis, but the Syrian government allowed the weapons to become available to Palestinian Arab *Fedayeen* terrorists, who in turn, in order to augment their treasury, and to abet terrorism in Ireland, had arranged to sell the weapons to I.R.A. agents.

Additional evidence that organised terrorism, the kind that is exported by the red-bloc nations, was also involved in Ireland, was made clear when it was discovered that Algerian terrorist-suppliers had bought 20 tons of weapons in Czechoslovakia for the I.R.A. in early 1972, the transaction being supervised by Soviet agents, specialists in revolutionary violence.

This kind of cooperation between terrorists abounds, and while it may not be the kind which semanticists would term 'centralised' or 'unified', it is nonetheless actual, strong, and on the increase, and it means, very simply, that there are no boundaries; Arab terrorists operating out of Syria, Jordan, Egypt, or Libya, monitor the progress of the I.R.A. in Ireland, including the very militant Provisional wing — or 'Provos' — who were responsible for the 'Bloody Friday' bombing in late July, 1972, which killed nine people and injured another 130, as well as the leftist official wing of the I.R.A. which is overtly pro-communist. In turn, there are links between the supposedly home-oriented Irish terrorists and additional foreign extremist organisations.

These people are professional destroyers, the ones operating inside Ireland and those supporting them from as far away as Egypt. They are not, however, the only outside suppliers. Americans have been contributing to the support of the outlaw Irish Republican Army through Irish-American organisations in the U.S. (several of them definitely leftist-controlled) to the extent of more than a half million dollars a year in cash, and U.S. intelligence sources are aware of quite extensive gun-running operations. In fact as late as 1972 indictments were returned by the U.S. Department of Justice against at least four subversive 'Provo' arms suppliers in the U.S. — two in California and two in New York. Also, investigations were under way in such divergent U.S. seaport areas as New England and the Gulf coast.

But not all these people were terrorists. In fact most of the cash contributions came from incensed Irish-Americans who were not leftists. But whether as manipulated dupes or as simply outraged sympathisers, they were conspicuously abetting terrorism through support of such organisations as the Irish Northern Aid Society, so in the end it amounted to the same thing. Eire's Prime Minister, John Lynch, offered a solution on a state visit to the United States in mid-January of 1973, when he suggested that Irish-Americans make their contributions through the official and non-partisan International Red Cross, which of course was well and good as far as it went, but could not be expected to influence those engaged in supplying armaments to Ireland's fighting factions.

Although there has been too much divergency among terrorists thus far to encourage an international, centralised committee for the direction of international terrorism, and at least in the foreseeable future this condition will continue to exist, nonetheless, there definitely is cooperation on an international scale, and the linkage making this possible is a common leftist philosophy.

Before the *Fedayeen* massacre of Israeli athletes at the XX Olympiad in Munich, many Western intelligence organisations had proof of this cooperation, but even if they had not learned as late as September 5th, when the Palestinian Black Septembrists struck in Munich, they would have had proof three months earlier when three youthful Japanese terrorists, members of Nippon's United Red Army (*Rengo Sekigun*) disembarked .at Lydda Airport from Air France Flight 132, and opened fire inside the crowded terminal with Czech VZT-58 automatic rifles, killing 26 unsuspecting people and wounding three times that many, for no apparent reason.

But of course there was a reason. The lone survivor among the Japanese gunman, Kozo Okamoto, who was tried and sentenced to life imprisonment for his part in the mass assassination, gave a version of the reason at his trial: "We are fighting a revolutionary war. Our war means assassinating people, destroying buildings and property. . . ." And in response to the bewildered query of an injured Puerto Rican pilgrim to the Holy Land, who wanted to known why Puerto Ricans were killed by a Japanese, because Arabs hated Israelis, the answer was simply that Japanese terrorists were no different from any other kind of terrorists; they recognised no boundaries in their war against society. In support of this, the Information Officer of the Popular Front for the Liberation of Palestine (P.F.L.P.), Ghassan Kanafani, announced shortly after the Lydda Airport bloodletting, that his organisation, the P.F.L.P., had sent the Japanese to Lydda "to kill as many people as possible".

Probing deeper for a connection between Japanese and Middle Eastern terrorists, turned up a bizarre sequence of events. For example, members of the *Rengo Sekigun* pirated an airliner more than two years prior to the Lydda Massacre and left it in North Korea, an armed bastion of Eastern communism. Subsequently, the North Korean capital of Pyongyang became a headquarters for the United Red Army.

As the North Korean arm of the *Rengo Sekigun* increased its outside activities, with North Korea's blessing, something it had not been allowed to do in Japan, other terrorists throughout the world took notice. Among the earlier arrivals at Rengo Sekigun headquarters in Pyongyang was Dr George Habash, erudite chieftain of the Popular Front for the Liberation of Palestine.

Between Habash and the violently uninhibited leaders of the United Red Army an arrangement was made whereby a number of Japanese members of the *Rengo Sekigun* would journey to P.F.L.P. training and staging camps in Jordan and Lebanon to be briefed and trained for terrorist strikes against Israel.

What ensued was the Lydda Massacre. As for Kozo Okamoto's involvement, he made it abundantly clear after being captured that it did not matter where, or against whom, terrorists would strike; the only important consideration was that members of organised, free societies, should be killed. He said there were other members of the United Red Army in training throughout the world to duplicate his accomplishment.

The same George Habash who went to Pyongyang to recruit Oriental anarchists for use in the Middle East, addressed a communist rally in North Korea in these words: ". . . there can be no political or geographical boundaries or moral limits to the operations of the people's camp." He also noted, quite truthfully, that ". . . in today's world, no one is innocent and no one is neutral."

If Habash's former statement were not significant for its assertion that terrorism, in his case communist-oriented terrorism, recognises no boundaries, his closing statement should have rather well epitomised this fact because it amounted to no less than an appeal to all terrorists to function through a unified effort. He already knew, as far back as 1968, that the Palestinian Arab terrorist organisations served as a rallying point for the alienated and disaffected from almost every nation in Europe, the Americas, and of course the Middle East; and Habash wanted that international cooperation to continue. It was reported that members of the Irish Republican Army and the radical U.S. Weathermen associations were present at the Lebanese and Jordanian *Fedayeen* training and indoctrination camps, where, according to a pro-Western intelligence source in Beirut, they were taught, among other terrorist skills, how to transport and utilise nitroglycerine, how to make 'letter-mines' (the American term for envelopes that explode, spraying shrapnel-like pellets when opened) and how to function efficiently as infiltratating assassins.

Even Turkey had terrorists in training at the *Fedayeen* camps, members of Turkey's Dev-Genc terrorist organisation. When Israel's Consul General in Turkey was assassinated in 1971, and a sudden and very energetic counter-move was unleashed by the Turkish government which resulted in the apprehension of a number of Dev-Genc terrorists, the authorities were informed by their captives that Consul-General Ephraim el-Ron had been slain as "part payment" for the *Fedayeen* training Turkish terrorists had received at the Palestinian Arab camps.

Also, as George Habash said in North Korea, there are no boundaries to terrorists, there are none where international cooperation is concerned either. When the female *Fedayeen* commando, Leila Khaled was captured subsequent to the abortive air pirating of an El Al aircraft on its way to London several years ago, and Israeli security agents on board killed her male companion, he was identified as one Patrick Arguello, a member of a Nicaraguan communist-terrorist organisation known as the *Tandanistas*. Except for a sympathetic affinity through terrorism, there could be no common ground between Tandanistas and Palestinian Arabs.

The leftist-terrorist policy of hands-across-the-border was additionally demonstrated in another bizarre way. The Czech-made VZT-58 automatic weapons used by Kozo Okamoto and his fellow assassins at Lydda Airport, were not given to the Japanese by Czech communists, they were supplied by Italian terrorists in Rome, where the Japanese flew from France, prior to their fateful arrival at Tel Aviv.

The German extremists who became internationally notorious for their terrorism as the Baader-Meinhof group, were trained at *Fedayeen* commando installations, and although both Andreas Baader and Ulrike Meinhof were apprehended by German police in mid-1972, their followers are still largely at liberty, awaiting, one may presume, new leaders, and otherwise as dedicated to murder, arson, and intimidation as ever. Genuine terrorists rarely retire, and even less often do they evince a change of either heart or politics.

Adding to the increasing power of the international terrorist apparatus is the fact that many nations, including of course such avowedly friendly ones as North Korea, North Vietnam, Cuba, Algeria, Libya, Syria and Egypt, as well as communist-controlled areas in such countries as Chile, Indonesia, Cambodia, Laos, to name a few, offer sanctuary to all terrorists.

Antoine Dahdahm of the Lebanese government summed up the international accord among terrorists from the viewpoint of a harrassed Establishment security official when he said: "International terrorists cannot help but meet and exchange ideas given the easy communications in the world today". He might have added that forged passports and other identification documents can be obtained quite simply in such liberal communities as Stockholm, Zurich, Brussels, Milan and Bordeaux in Europe, and also in every Middle Eastern country where pan-Arabism and anti-Israelism is extant, as well as in no less than fifteen nations of the western hemisphere including the United States where forged documents of any kind can be bought quite inexpensively in both New York and San Francisco. London, where forged documents of identity can no doubt be procured also, enjoys a unique position among terrorists. As Switzerland and Portugal have been regarded as essentially centres of neutrality during European wars, London holds that same unique position among international terrorists. In London, extremists are seldom troubled by the authorities providing they remain orderly and are not subject to extradition as individuals wanted elsewhere by nations with whom the British have extradition treaties. Probably because cosmopolitan London offers advantages not found elsewhere – for example on the Continent in Paris, Madrid or Berlin – extremism by foreign terrorists is practically unheard of in London, excluding the I.R.A.

European cities avoided by terrorists have been most generally in Spain and Portugal. In the Americas the least hospitable cities have been Mexico City, Managua, and Guatemala City, in the south, and Edmonton, Winnipeg, and Lethbridge, in Canada, while in the United States there are no *large* cities of the size of Chicago, Cincinnati, Los Angeles or San Francisco which can be classified as inhospitable to extremists, although there are innumerable smaller communities, like those of lower Southern California (in Orange and Riverside Counties) which are hostile not only to terrorists, but even to liberal students, teachers and politicians.

In consequence, then, whatever the reason — sympathy, affinity, or neutrality — international terrorism has become as mobile as any other facet of society. Moreover, it has a large number of active proponents serving its cause throughout the world as officers or attaches at the numerous leftist embassies and consuls. One, at least, an accredited official of Democratic Yemen, with headquarters in Switzerland, is his nation's liaison official with the United Nations. His name is Daoud Barakat, and he is thought in several reliable Intelligence quarters to have been the man who planned the Munich Massacre of Israelis at the XX Olympiad in early September of 1972. He is known to be affiliated with the Black September Palestinian Arab *Fedayeen* movement, which carried out that deadly affair.

There can remain little doubt but that international terrorism, whether of the Moscow-oriented variety, or of the totally militant, anarchic kind advocated at the Trotskyite Fourth International Convention in Brussels in 1970, which advocated even the overthrow of the Soviets, or whether it is the sectional terrorism most Arabs and Irish believe in, has become a world force. It has not become a world power, and it could not be a world force if those who oppose it knew how to counteract it, but they either do not know, or are fearful of the repercussions certain to follow in the wake of reprisals in kind.

When Israel struck back after the Munich Olympiad Affair, using warplanes, rockets, and bombs which resulted in the death of a number of presumably innocent Arab villagers, along with a number of genuine *Fedayeen* terrorists, the international reaction was swift and denunciatory. Even within Israel itself there were voices raised in protest. All of this signified that society was unwilling to use the tools of exorcism against terrorists, these extremists used against society, which appear to be the only tools currently at hand which the terrorists respect and which society has available to it.

Conceivably, in the future, something superior to violence for both sides will be discovered, but in the 1950s, the 1960s and at present in the 1970s, no such happy solutions seems to be available.

Violent terrorism, which fattens on every variety of discontent, whether genuine or not, has been employed by irresponsible demagogues and has also been assimilated by millions of impressionable people. When an American negro named David Hilliard, of the militant Black Panther Party, said, "We will kill Richard Nixon", he was planting the thought in hundreds of minds, of which only one need seek to implement that pronouncement, or, if that one fails, then another can seek to implement it, or another and still another, until at length the reverberation of the statement will succeed in achieving an accomplishment.

Terrorism actually goes beyond the limits, and probably beyond the control, of disciplined leftists. The Trotskyites, for example, are not dedicated to the establishment of world communism as it is generally propounded by its international followers. Extreme terrorism usually focuses on a particular target in a particular country, its adherents concentrating to the exclusion of all else, including ideology, upon their goal. This may be, as Colonel Antoine Dahdahm, previously cited, says, "not a real threat to security" but Dahdahm was undoubtedly correct when he also said, "it is definitely a new problem that will make terrorism much harder to predict and control."

Actually, activist guerrillas of both varieties, communist indoctrinated and controlled, or the pure nihilists who believe terrorism is the end as well as the means, serve in the same anti-social, anti-Establishment counter-culture, and this does not lessen the peril, because of their divergence or disunity — it enhances it.

The violently radical Brazilian, Carlos Marighella, who was shot to death in 1969 in a police ambush, exhorted all terrorists when he said that "the urban guerrilla's only reason for existence . . . is to shoot."

For the dedicated terrorist, whatever his motivation, whether it is nihilistic, nationalistic, ideological, racial or social, whether he believes he is a 'soldier' in the great cause of regenerating mankind, or simply seeks redress for some iniquity, the oldtime dream of the Bolshevik, that he will live to see a new and shining world, no longer applies.

For the past half generation extremists have been exalted to the role of sainted martyrs, have been exhorted not to expect to witness the establishment of Utopia, if such an establishment is possible, but to serve as zealots in the destruction of all evil.

What, then, can such people identify with, beyond destruction and perhaps, fundamentally, their own 'heroic' death?

Kozo Okamoto, the surviving mass-murder of Lydda Airport, told his captor that he felt a strange ecstasy as people fell dead and dying around him. He was convinced from the much earlier beginning of his undertaking that, one way or another, his life was forfeit.

Terrorists such as Kozo Okamoto serve systems — leftist or rightist, nationalist or nihilist — but only because everyone, even those who seek hardest to destroy society, must function within the confines of an organisation which is, like it or not, a segment of society. But the real terrorist has never been a complete ally of any system, and the deeper his terrorist motivation runs, the less genuine subservience is in him. Since the triumph of the Bolshevik Revolution in 1917, no employer of terrorists has known this better than the communists. The first to go to the wall when communism has triumphed in the past, have been the terrorists.

At best terrorism creates disunity and encourages anti-forces. At worst, it is a spectacular, short-lived career or vocation. The terrorist is as much of a threat to those he serves as those he opposes. More than two generations ago the Soviets learned that those to whom terrorism is the standard reaction against anything they do not approve of, cannot be integrated into an organised society, let alone a disciplined, or regimented society.

THREE

The Fedayeen

Until recently there existed in Iran a completely negative, reactionary force of archaists called the *Fadayane Eslam*. Its members opposed westernisation in any form, despised Jews, loathed all foreigners, hated Armenians, opposed liberal education, rejected female emancipation, and throve on anarchy, violence and terror.

No one who opposes female emancipation can be all bad; nevertheless, the *Fadayane* were virtually obliterated when the Iranian government moved to destroy them, in the process killing their chieftan Navvab Safavi.

What the *Fadayane* best represented was the depth of unreasoning hatred Arabs were capable of. Historically, Islam has produced, and has been renowned for, some unusually violent and unappeasable Arabs. But Islam has also produced the immortal Salah-eh-Din-Yussuf-Ibn-Ayub, who did not, like Mohammed, experience great difficulty in maintaining a reasoning posture of moderation on such subjects as Islamic law, faith, and lands.

Anyone, from the century of the Crusaders to the present day who violated, slighted, or insulted all three, was faced with the kind of implacable obduracy that no amount of conciliation could ever appease.

If that violator were a Jew, first-cousin of all Arabs, as well as Islam's particular, historically despised foe, then there was no hope at all for conciliation. A truce, perhaps, but never — for as long as Islam stood and had one hand to strike with — peace.

If the loathsome Jew were supported by Christian wealth, power and arms, and, employing this formidable advantage, took Arab land and in the process killed Moslems, he committed the most thoroughly and everlastingly unpardonable desecration one enemy could perpetrate against another.

Israel did exactly that, not only in the relatively recent Six Day War – an unspeakable humiliation throughout Islam – but earlier, between May of 1948 and July of 1949, when the Israelis in their first conflict as a unified nation, triumphed over the Arab League. In the process of both those conflicts, which were separated by almost two decades of armed restraint and active terrorism by both sides, they acquired and refused to relinquish a rather considerable amount of Arab land, and in the course of this acquisition, created the homeless and destitute Palestinian Arab whose property was expropriated, whose livelihood was taken away from him, and who became an outcast in his own hereditary land. He also became heir to the unique propensity for hatred that has made Arab animosity and vengeance avoided in both Europe and Africa since the end of the Crusades, seven hundred years ago.

In the Arab world the Palestinian Arab outcast has been known as the *Fedayeen,* meaning 'they who sacrifice themselves', and in their fanatical implacability they became the very appropriate successors to Iran's older brotherhood of *Fadayane Eslam.* They did not undertake total war against Israel for the return of their homeland, although this has been generally the understanding Europeans and Americans have of their aims. They were and remain, totally and fanatically dedicated to the destruction of Israel; restoration of their expropriated lands, if it occurred tomorrow, would not culminate in a very noticable depreciation in their *jehad,* their holy war. They have existed only to kill Jews and destroy the Jewish state.

The majority of *Fedayeen* have been young; it was their parents who were dispossessed back in 1948. They matured in the filth, squalor, and rancour of refugee camps, learning to survive by deceit and theft, and became in time implacable haters of the West and Israel.

The older people existed in apathy without work, hope, or self-respect, but as the younger Palestinian Arabs matured, they had to face a legacy of scorn, even from other Arabs. They were able to place the blame where it belonged; and having nothing to lose, they could only win, by becoming anti-Zion terrorists.

Of course they were easy and willing subjects for any ideology that offered them encouragement, but even so, when Soviet agitators appeared with weapons, funds, and most cherished of all, a means for gaining self-respect, although the ragged and hungry *Fedayeen* almost without exception identified with this new ally, many of them did not do so as converts, even though they employed red-line rhetoric, but took advantage of an expediency. Their fanatacism, by the 1960s and 1970s, had become too thoroughly embedded, too entirely oriented towards their own uniquely Islamic function to allow room for serving another master. They would accept any aid and any ally including the pseudo-sympathetic Soviets, if that was what would be required to destroy Israel.

They were, and remain, completely dedicated to terrorism, and like the Trotskyites, concentrate every effort towards destruction. They have not promulgated plans to be implemented after victory. They are fanatical terrorists, but they are not naive; the chances for those currently involved in *jehad* to survive and witness the defeat of the West by no more than 2 ½ million displaced Palestinian Arabs, of whom no more than perhaps 20,000 are fighting *Fedayeen*, are so slight as to be non-existent.

But there was a way: create a situation of detente between the West and the Soviet Union, then manufacture an incident which would precipitate world war. An alternative was to interest the Soviet Union, which does not favour Israel either, to support a united Arab effort to conquer Jordan, whose borders are contiguous with Israel, and thus help establish in Jordan a *Fedayeen* state. There was reason such a plan might succeed: Jordan's population was at least half Palestinian; Amman, the capital, had a population three-quarters made up of Palestinians. It was thought King Hussein's army — mostly Bedouin tribesmen from the east bank of the Jordan River — could not possibly withstand a Soviet-sponsored attack by both *Fedayeen* fighters and the Syrian army, which could be used to spearhead the invasion (entirely controlled by Soviet officers as advisors to battalion level) while at the same time being stabbed in the back by Jordanian Palestinians.

It was an excellent plan. Hussein's army, tough and resourceful though it was, could not in all probability have prevented the fall of

Jordan. *Fedayeen* strategists, Soviet agitators, and Syrian military officers agreed on the details in early September, 1970. When clearance from Moscow was received — the Soviet officers with the Syrian invasion force were not to cross the Jordanian border — a very quiet period of preparation began. The Russians were to remain well in the background. The world was to be presented with a view of another eruption of trouble in the chronically-troubled Middle East, which would not pose a threat to London, Paris, or Washington.

Victory, which seemed almost certain, would have overthrown Jordan's very capable and politically moderate King Hussein, replacing him with a Soviet controlled *Fedayeen* 'people's republic' dedicated to the defeat and dismemberment of Israel.

This *Fedayeen*-supported, three-party subterfuge could not, of course, have remained a secret long. What followed, without two-thirds of the world realising it, and with no more than a handful of Americans having any inkling of it at all, was the most chilling confrontation between the two superpowers, the U.S. and the U.S.S.R., since the Cuban Missile Crisis which had occurred almost a decade earlier.

Intelligence reports alerted Washington. On 21st September, Washington contacted Israel's ambassador and was informed that the Israelis were aware of what was underway in Syria and among the *Fedayeen*, and felt entirely capable of handling it by turning back the Syrian force before it could reach Amman — providing that the United States, Israel's ally, would prevent Soviet support of the Syrians. U.S. President Nixon agreed. Later, when the U.S. Department of State advocated a diplomatic approach to Moscow, President Nixon declined, and the U.S. elite 82nd Airborne Division in Germany was alerted for possible combat duty, the U.S. Sixth Fleet in the Mediterranean was reinforced and placed on war-footing, the Greek government was requested to permit a staging area to be established for the use of troops subject to combat in the Middle East, and on 22nd September, Soviet intelligence officers read the signs correctly and Yuli Vorentsov of the Soviet embassy in Washington hastened to the State Department for an explanation. He was informed that the Soviet-supported Syrian invasion of Jordan had better not reach Amman.

But the Syrian tanks and armoured units were already moving, and the *Fedayeen* had begun guerilla attacks inside Jordan. Frantic orders went out from the Soviets. As the Jordanian army moved against the attacking armour, the foremost Syrian tank abruptly changed course and led the ignominious withdrawal which followed.

The Syrians returned to their homeland, the Soviets abandoned the guerilla *Fedayeen* terrorists still fighting in Jordan, Amman's Palestinians had no opportunity to stab King Hussein's army in the back; and although the Jordanian army did not achieve a clear-cut victory in the confused and prolonged skirmishing which continued to rage in Jordan subsequent to the Soviet-Syrian withdrawal, King Hussein was not overthrown. Israel did nto have to march, and if there was no triumph for the Jordanians, neither was there one for the fanatical *Fedayeen*.

The other alternative remained, and in fact still remains; a deliberate, calculated crisis which could precipitate serious trouble between those who support the *Fedayeen*, and those who support Israel.

Generally, though, *Fedayeen* strategy has not been on this scale. There have been joint, or cooperative, efforts between the leftist Syrians and the *Fedayeen* before, and in fact it could be reasonably assumed that the Palestinians would cooperate with anyone who pronounced against Israel, but most commonly their terrorism has been of the more direct, physical kind.

The murder of Israel's athletes at Munich was carried out by the Black September wing of the *Fedayeen Al Fatah* organisation (*fatah* means 'victory' in Arabic). There were a number of other federated or subsidiary *Fedayeen* groups, some very secret, some less or more fanatical, and while they did not all recognise the supremacy of *Al Fatah's* chieftan Yassar Arafat, they did cooperate in such causes as terrorist attacks upon Israel, and in the 1970 fighting in Jordan.

Al Fatah has probably very close to 10,000 armed men at call, peak strength, but Yassar Arafat, who is not known as a fanatic, does not receive full homage from the extremists. He appears to be slightly left of centre, but not a communist, although he had been feted in both Hanoi and Peking.

What does not quite endear Arafat to the terrorists is his occasional moderation. For example, he has said that he does not seek the destruction of the Jews, only their Zionist state, the implication seeming to be that he would welcome a return of all Arab lands to their former owners, and perhaps a separate enclave called Israel, Arab-dominated of course, but with a multi-ethnic population, including Jews.

This is not what the *Fedayeen* seek, and it is not what they will settle for, and to ensure that their strength will continue, they have taken over refugee camps, installed their own political cadre-men, and are indoctrinating Palestinian children as young as eight years of age; those a little older, fifteen and sixteen years of age, are assigned to active guerrilla units. All are trained with the *Fedayeen's* favourite weapon, the Soviet-made Balashnikov automatic rifle, but there are also training courses involving other handguns, as well as many different kinds of bombs, rockets and grenades. A popular *Fedayeen* weapon has been the Russian Katyusha rocket, which can travel a considerable distance, and which has the additional advantage of responding efficiently to a timing device that does not fire the rocket until the terrorists are well away.

These are not the things, however, with which the Palestinians hope to drive the Israelis into the sea. They are the means by which they hope to decimate them in their *jehad* of attrition which they vow to continue for a generation or more, until something more opportune appears — hopefully, to them, a decline in U.S. strength, a dissolution of the North Atlantic Treaty Organisation (NATO), or possibly, a greater role in the Middle East by the Soviet Union.

Meanwhile, they maintain training and staging camps in Jordan, Lebanon and elsewhere. They infiltrate past Israeli outposts by night to plant mines, commit assassinations — very often of Arabs who work with, or conduct business with, Israelis — send terrorists like Kozo Okamoto to kill as many Israelis as possible, and to create incidents of international impact such as the Munich Massacre.

They have also begun to cause reaction in some Arab quarters. For example, after the murder of Israel's eleven Olympic athletes in Munich, Israeli retaliation was devastating. Air strikes at *Fedayeen* camps, perhaps inevitably, resulted in the death by bombing of a number of innocent Arab villagers. After the bloody Lydda Airport affair, Israeli secret agents killed the P.F.L.P.'s information officer,

Ghassan Kanafani, by wiring the ignition of his car to a swatch of dynamite sticks secured beneath the vehicle. There were other retaliatory acts, all of them savage, swift, and obviously designed to drive home the point, which was, very simply, that for every *Fedayeen* outrage perpetrated against Israelis, the Arab world could expect payment in kind, with interest.

But this has not caused a lessening of terrorist attacks. It has however, encouraged among some Arab leaders, a particular wariness towards the *Fedayeen*, but after the ignominy of the 1967 Arab-Israeli War, Arab leaders have not dared denounce the *Fedayeen*. It is upon these selfless fanatics that Islam's hopes for reversing that terrible humiliation rests. Not the leaders; some of them, including Egypt's wily politician Anwar Sadat, whose thunderous proclamation and miniscule actions are designed purely to placate both sides, are perfectly aware what another Arab-Israeli armed clash could do — topple them from power. They are also aware that they have nothing with which to counteract Israel's secret weapon: the Israeli has to die where he stands because he has no other place to go. That kind of determination, coupled to superior strategy, cannot be beaten, except by the equal fanaticism of the *Fedayeen*, but he is not strong enough, and his Arab allies, such as the Egyptians and Syrians, do not possess his kind of unalterable resolution. In fact, the *Fedayeen* could do better to take as allies almost anyone else. Syria has not been a worthwhile ally for anyone in almost a thousand years, and the Egyptians never were.

Meanwhile, the *Fedayeen* fight on. Their terrorism has gone far beyond Israel's borders. Ami Shachori, the agricultural attache at Israel's London embassy, opened a letter postmarked Amsterdam in his Kensington office in late 1972, and detonated a "letter mine" which killed him. An airliner bound for Israel from Switzerland was destroyed in mid-air by a time-bomb with a loss of forty-seven lives. In the spring of 1972 a German Lufthansa airliner was skyjacked after leaving New Delhi, bound for Frankfort, with a crew of fourteen, and 171 passengers, by five *Fedayeen* armed with grenades and pistols. The aircraft was diverted to Aden in leftist South Yemen where a demand was made upon the West Germans for 5 million dollars ransom for both passengers and the airplane, a Boeing 747.

A courier was sent to a rendezvous near Beirut where the ransom was paid, after which the aircraft and its passengers and crewmen were allowed to continue their journey. One of the passengers was the 19-year-old son of the late Senator Robert F. Kennedy, assassinated by an Arab, Sirhan Bishara Sirhan, in 1968. South Yemen allowed the sky pirates to leave unharmed. West German Transport Minister George Leber said the sky piracy was clearly "the work of an international group with worldwide contacts".

Near the end of February, 1972, *Fedayeen* terrorists killed three more Israelis in the bloody and ceaseless guerilla fighting that has not diminished despite Israeli retaliation, over the past half dozen years, and more. Retaliation, as usual, was swift and harsh as Israeli armour and aircraft struck hard at Palestinian staging areas in Lebanon, close to Israel's frontier.

Terrorism and retaliation continued, and still continues. In late September, 1972, 60 Palestinians and 40 Lebanese were killed in an Israeli retaliation attack, and the Lebanese leaders finally came out favouring some kind of limitation on terrorists operating out of the *Al Fatah*-controlled southern territories of Lebanon. Syria, equally hard hit in Israeli retaliatory attacks, also wanted some kind of limitation put upon the *Fedayeen*, although the great Arab majority considered talk of this kind as near-treason. In fact, *Fedayeen* heroes, armed and swaggering, appeared even in King Hussein's capital of Amman, confident that they would not be molested. Nor were they, despite the bitterness Jordan's army felt towards them.

They died often, as did the killers of the Israeli athletes at Munich, but they did not die easily. They were prepared to die. Many terrorist units that have infiltrated past Israeli guard-positions at night have lost as many as one-half their number in bombing, assassination, arson and machine-gun attacks upon both Israeli army posts and civilian communities.

Four Palestinians, members of the deadly Black September Organisation, deliberately pirated a Sabena aircraft en route from Brussels to Tel Aviv in mid-May 1972, and had the aircraft land at Lydda Airport, in the very heartland of their enemies. Knowing, as they had reason to know from long experience, that the Israelis could not be bluffed, those four *Fedayeen*, two men and two women, then engaged in a 23-hour-long negotiation with Israel's top officials including Defence Minister Moshe Dayan. The only security for the *Fedayeen* were their hostages, 87 passengers and 10 crewmen. But these were no guarantee. Israeli security agents went in as 'service men' to refuel the airplane. Instead, they deflated the tyres, emptied the fuel tanks, and disabled the pressurising system. Meanwhile, the terrorists gave the Israeli authorities a list of 319 Arab terrorists being held in Israel for whom they would exchange their hostages.

An elite unit of Israeli commandos dressed as aircraft maintenance men, armed with pistols and knives charged the aircraft, flung open its doors, cried out for the passengers to lie down, and engaged the Palestinians in a gun battle. One woman air pirate was shot and gravely injured, the other woman threw herself down and cried out over and over, "I surrender, I surrender." Both of the male Black.Septembrists were shot to death.

Eight others were wounded, two Israeli commandos and six of the terrified passengers. An Israeli spokesman said there had never, from the very beginning, been any intention of acceding to the *Fedayeen's* demand. Nor, it was affirmed later, would Israel ever yield, no matter what the risks or the consequences, to this kind of blackmail.

The Palestinians who pirated Sabena Flight 571, Brussels to Tel Aviv, did not have a chance of succeeding, something they surely suspected. Israel had steadfastly refused every other similar demand for the release of Arab terrorists, including the one made by the Munich Black Septembrists who killed the eleven Israeli athletes during the Olympic games, and were subsequently killed themselves — all but three — by German security agents.

The *Fedayeen* have proved themselves to be merciless and fanatical. But they have also emerged as clever, knowledgeable and tactically sophisticated activists who employ the latest terrorist tools and tactics. Ideologically, they are leftist and indoctrinated, but realistically they remain what they have always been — implacable anti-Zionist terrorists who will cooperate with any other organisation of guerrilla extremists in the world; and this of course makes them part of the loosely controlled but world-wide association of international terrorists.

FOUR

Some Techniques Of Terrorism

Not all terrorists are leftists, but all of them employ the rhetoric and techniques which leftists have been perfecting over the past half-century and longer. In Western nations such as France, Great Britain and the United States, and such nations as Japan, South Vietnam, Indonesia and the Philippines, in the East, the customary procedure among terrorists has followed a subtle but recognisable strategy. Firstly, violent and seemingly irresponsible acts of terrorism are committed against established authority; social, academic, political or police-authority. Secondly, the perpetrators of these acts allow themselves to be apprehended, ideally while newspaper and television cameras are photographing mass arrests. Thirdly, these 'victims' of authoritarian (police) force, i.e., 'fascist power', are 'brutally abused'.

Up to this point sympathy has commonly been elicited for the 'victims' among all classes of people who may have had their own unpleasant experiences with police – or with any uniformed authority.

The next step has been to try and rally all those sympathetic people in one place, either under the pretext of hearing the celebrated 'victims' denounce the horrors they have survived, or by simply inviting everyone to a music-rock-festival. When these rallies have succeeded, as many have, the aggregate has quite often numbered many thousands, or more people than most metropolitan police forces could adequately cope with. The news media has been invited, often being given special treatment, particularly cameramen.

The next step has been to stage a dramatic 'incident'. This was at once blamed upon the police, especially, but to compel the police, who have limited facilities for controlling large crowds, to appeal for reinforcements. Troops, (commonly National Guardsmen in the U.S.) have been called out and cameras recorded the club-swinging police in action as steel-helmeted troops, bayonets in place, moved up in support of the police . . .

It has happened exactly this way innumerable times from New York to Tokyo. The strategy has been to use a large gathering of people as a lever to compel the calling out of troops, which inevitably antagonises everyone including television audiences, across the country and overseas, who know only that armed soldiers have been used against unarmed civilians.

Everything which has occurred up to this point has been designed to create confusion, disunity, and antagonism. A small cadre of professional terrorists, numbering perhaps less than fifty people, has successfully aroused a crowd numbering many thousands, has promoted disharmony throughout a large city, and disunity through an entire nation.

Nor does it end there. To arouse the crowd, the community and the nation, has, according to professional cadre-men, proved gratifyingly easy; but a greater and more subtle effort is required to sustain the agitation, and one method among many corollary options available to terrorists, has been 'police brutality'. Not the allegation but the fact of police brutality. The subtlety emerges in the manner by which this is accomplished.

Hardcore terrorists, very often young girls especially selected for their wholesome appearance before newscasting television cameras, are taught how to use their feet and knees, which are below camera-level, to strike policemen in either the shins or the groin. All terrorist cademen are drilled in methods of secret attack, most of which are not camera-detectable, such as stabbing policemen with long hatpin-like needles, or using small palm-sized syringe-type rubber bulbs filled with ammonia. They are taught to provoke retaliation first, then to scream and writhe as the police apprehend them, very often clubbing them, and while the terrorists' initial provocation is almost never recorded, police retaliation *is* recorded because the terrorists make certain that it will be, and, providing that the terrorists have properly staged their demonstration, it can be expected that a national outcry against police brutality will ensue.

In some countries this sequence of events has snowballed, resulting in civilian outrage, increased indignation, larger and more violent demonstrations against authority, which have ensured more police, more troops, military armour, and governments have fallen, as inconceivable as it may seem, because a small, well-disciplined nucleus of terrorists were more skilful at dividing and destroying a nation than other men have been at preventing its destruction.

Some years ago this strategy was tried in the U.S., at Kent State University in Ohio, and succeeded surprisingly well in creating a nation-wide outraged uproar. It did not go beyond the initial stages because it lacked sustaining power; when the troops fired into the crowd, something which was not actually anticipated even by the most radical terrorists, the shock created a vacuum. By the time the cadre-men recovered sufficiently to re-assert leadership, the central impetus was lost. But in other countries, it has succeeded; in the Phillippines, terrorists have forced a complete suspension of free, democratic processes; in Mexico terrorism has compelled the government to use dictatorial powers of suppression, and in Japan terrorists have encouraged the founding of anti-terrorist execution squads.

In leftist countries, the techniques of terrorism do not succeed. In those communities, where the tactics of terrorism originated, aside from the repression that is inherent in leftism, as the strategies were perfected, defenses against them were likewise perfected. The youth of leftist countries have been expertly manipulated; have been duped into seeking to export terrorism, and, as in the case of Cuba, have been so successfully deluded that they are uncompromisingly convinced no system is the equal of their system, but above all else, youth yearns for *causes*, for physical participation, for personal involvement. A cause has never, historically, had to possess merit to appeal to the young; all it has ever had to have was a willingness to allow the young to actively and physically participate.

Sixty-seven years ago Nikolai Lenin wrote: "Go to the youth, form fighting squads everywhere of 3, 10, 30 persons. Let them arm themselves as best they can, be it with a revolver, a knife . . . you must proceed to propagandize on a large scale. Let 5 or 10 per cent make the rounds of hundreds of workers and student study circles, and supply each group with brief and simple recipes for making bombs . . . kill a spy or blow up a police station . . . raid a bank to confiscate money for the insurrection . . . Let every group learn, if only by beating up policemen . . ."

"Beating up policemen . . ." In the entire decade prior to 1970 rarely were more than a dozen U.S. policemen killed annually, but during the years 1970, 1971, and 1972 the death-rate among policemen slain by terrorist-guerillas exceeded 100 victims per year. Prior to the 1960-1970 decade, indiscriminate and wanton police killings were rare, subsequently, policemen were hunted, deliberately stalked as though they were wild game, most of them being killed from ambush. In one month, December of 1972, 13 U.S. policemen were stalked and shot to death without reason or warning, not in the process of making apprehensions, but from ambush, slain by assassins.

In early January, 1973, a black terrorist named Mark James Essex whose middle-class, respectable parents lived in Emporia, Kansas, barricaded himself on the top of a hotel in New Orleans, possibly with accomplices, although only Essex remained to be identified, and shot it out with the New Orleans police department in a battle which lasted 32 hours.

Prior to his shooting spree, Essex, who was 23 years old, told a maid in the hotel where the skirmish occurred, "The revolution's here." Before Essex died from marksmen's gunfire, plus some rounds from a U.S. Marine Corps helicopter gunship's machine gun, 21 people had been wounded, and 7 had been killed, of whom 3 were policemen.

Mark James Essex was not a leftist although among his effects found after his death there were a number of leftist pamphlets and scribbled quotations. Essex was an embittered, youthful, emotionally unstable advocate of 'black power'. Leftism's encouragement of violence was tailored to Essex's emotional instability and his bitterness. It served him exactly as it has served youthful Palestinian Arabs, but it would be a mistake to write off Mark James Essex as a communist. He was a terrorist; more properly a guerilla-terrorist, and recognition of this fact emerged in the aftermath of the Essex tragedy, when William Guste, attorney general for the state of Louisiana, said, "I am convinced that there is an underground national suicidal group bent on creating terror in America."

But obviously there is nothing exclusively American about this terrorist underground, and its techniques are not entirely suicidal, although hard evidence indicates that suicide-groups are certainly no small part of international terrorism. Nikolai Lenin spelled it out almost seventy years ago; people like Mark James Essex, among a host of other bombers, snipers, ambushers-of-police, mob-manipulaters, and some quite sophisticated and undeniably clever leadership cliques, have been implementing Lenin's dictums ever since, but not entirely as communists, although they have certainly taken every advantage of leftism's advocacy of violent terrorism. Communism, however, has indubitably been the motivation for a great number of these people.

There is in fact a large and constantly increasing world-wide underground federation, or association, of terrorists. In America, a black man such as Mark James Essex could find more reason, or at least different reasons, to wish to destroy the 'system' than could a white American terrorist; but the end result in either case would be the same, and, going farther afield in seeking corollaries one might assume that a black socio-path in New Orleans was not altogether different from machine-gun-firing Japanese terrorists in Tel Aviv. Even though the Japanese were members of the *Rengo Sekigun* (United Red Army) and the black youth in New Orleans scribbled leftist mottoes, the suicidal acts of these people were, first and foremost, terroristic, and secondly, socio-political. They could not, and did not, change anything, but they could and did emphasise the increasing power of terrorism in the modern world. The best proof that terrorism for its own sake has achieved a maturing status will be evinced when terrorists strike within the Soviet Union, an event which seems almost inevitable, and which will certainly support the contention that although terrorists employ old-line Bolshevik rhetoric, their war is against all 'establishments', not just those varieties endemic in democratic societies.

Lenin's directive to "supply each group with brief and simple recipes for making bombs" has over the decades encouraged one of the foremost terrorist techniques, not only in bomb-devastated Ireland, but elsewhere. A classical recent example would be the mid-May 1972 bombing of the world's largest office building, the U.S. Pentagon.

Ten sticks of dynamite and a simple delayed action timing device were secreted in a ladies' rest-room on the fourth floor, which, by no mistake, happened to be directly above the ultra-secret strategy-planning chamber of the U.S. Joint Chiefs of Staff, perhaps in the hope that the world's most powerful military leaders might be convening downstairs, when the bomb detonated.

They were not; the explosion occurred shortly before dawn when only stand-by crews were on duty in the building, none near the fourth-floor ladies' lounge, where a gaping 30-foot hole was torn in the reinforced cement wall, and windows were smashed elsewhere.

Scarcely had the echoes died when a radical-terrorist U.S. underground organisation known as the 'Weathermen' took credit for the bombing stating that the attack had been planned to coincide with what would have been the 82nd birthday of North Vietnam's late premier, Ho Chi Minh.

The 'Weathermen' were avowed leftists. All their previous acts of terrorism were communist-oriented or inspired. These people were never suicidal; they were instead calculatingly deadly and whole-heartedly dedicated to hardcore leftism. They were never recklessly terroristic, and one could reasonably assume that this has been the basic difference between genuine leftists and genuine terrorists. The communists have rarely gone suicidally all-out, but the terrorists have never avoided all-out suicidal commitment.

Elsewhere Lenin's "simple recipes for making bombs" provided terrorists with what became their most formidable weapon. It has also provided hospitals and morgues with a steady supply of the dying and the dead from Belfast to Tel Aviv and from Khartoum to Milan. In recent years terrorist bombings in the U.S., besides the toll in dead and maimed, have done damage in excess of 25 million dollars but the greatest and most appalling toll from bombings which have occurred in recent years, has taken place in Ireland where, between August, 1969 and January, 1973, minimal estimates of damage have placed the monetary cost of destruction in excess of 100 million dollars, which in view of the smallness of the country, is devastating. This does not take into consideration the cost in human lives, nor in human suffering. Nor does such an estimate suggest that Ireland's agonisingly prolonged guerilla conflict is anywhere close to a conclusion.

The techniques of terror which have been perfected elsewhere, notably in leftist lands, have found a proving-ground in Northern Ireland, but not only there; an entire portfolio of world-wide grievances have encouraged the spread of active terrorism. People, such as the nationalist French-Canadians, too ownership-oriented to be good communists, have employed terrorist tactics, from fire-bombs to taking and executing hostages, to wiring mailboxes, cars, even to sniping at police. In Italy, France, in areas of Africa as well as in North, Central and South America, terrorism, and terrorist tactics, have proliferated beyond most expectations, within the past two decades. Printed manuals on terrorism are commonly available, the uninformed as well as the misinformed still see in each terrorist a communist saboteur, and this, more than anything else, is a fair guage of just how much genuine ignorance presently exists respecting terrorism.

Orderly people have never been satisfied with the simple statement that the Devil is loose; they have sought a red herring, and unless they have found one, they have manufactured one. This is understandable, but as a matter of fact the growth and spread of terrorism, as, for example in current Ireland and the Middle East — although most certainly profiting from communism's oldtime Bolshevik ethos, and mouthing leftism's rhetoric — is actually much more likely to be based upon indigenous social issues, such as Catholic versus Protestant, Arab versus Israeli, black versus white, poor versus rich.

The techniques which have been developed, generally through physical utility, have become infinitely more sophisticated than they once were, and there is good reason to expect their sophistication to become even more specialised; for example, the people who penetrated the Pentagon's exceptionally elaborate protective system, known to be among the best in the world, are the same people who could, with a lot less expertise, infiltrate the drinking-water facilities of any large city and, through utilisation of either outright toxics, or virulent disease cultures, make a very great number of people very ill.

Thus, the techniques of terrorism have improved, and will continue to improve, and in general, orderly taxpaying people will continue to react with outrage at what they predominantly believe is an international communist conspiracy — and which to a great extent actually was such a conspiracy, once, but which is no longer. The Devil *is* loose; he does not bear aloft a red banner emblazoned with a hammer and sickle — not exclusively, at any rate — nor is he required to explain his motivation in comprehensible terms, and if he tried, the wealth-generating systemics would neither accept what he told them, nor believe what he told them. This would be, basically, that an entire fresh variety of social disease has evolved from the transitional social culture of a rapidly changing world, and no one is doing anything about it — except the terrorists — and if this would not appear to justify terrorism in the eyes of those who sustain and support the system, it most certainly would appear to the terrorists as a valid reason for what they are doing.

As for leftism — it is no longer the fresh, bright hope it once was for most malcontents. The reactionary, cautiously conservative Supreme Presidium of the Soviet Union has not been the social or political lode-stone of terrorists in many years. Even the most recent upheavals within the People's Republic of China have not provided answers for people who now see freedom as in no way related to regimentation, and those who persist in the ways of archaic leftism — as for example America's 'Weathermen' — will simply atrophy; the pace of change is too fast, the basic issues are changed, and are still changing. Terrorism for its own sake, has come of age. Even if the basic causes were acknowledged and steps were taken to correct the wrongs, how could they be changed? Israel will not yield an acre of Arab land to the Palestinians; America's power-structure will not cut off its own right hand, which is the one holding fast to enormous corporate and political leverage; Japan's industrialists will not acknowledge let alone move to correct, their piranha-like overseas blood-sucking — meanwhile terrorism flourishes. It will continue to do so, throughout the world — not to force change — terrorists have never been very hopeful. They have learned to thrive on an elemental factor in human nature — hatred, not hope. So — the Devil *is* loose!

'World revolution' is a phrase, like the phrase 'endemic irregularity'. One has just as much validity behind it as the other. To those who serve terrorism, and who are total pragmatists, there is another term which categorises both of these terms, and which is equally devoid of meaning — that wonderfully Christian word 'hope'.

The Munich Olympiad,
September 1972: a member
of the Hong Kong team
jumps from his apartment
in the building where Arab
terrorists were holding
thirteen Israeli hostages

The Lydda Airport massacre,
May 1972: an airport
employee picks up a victim's
shoe

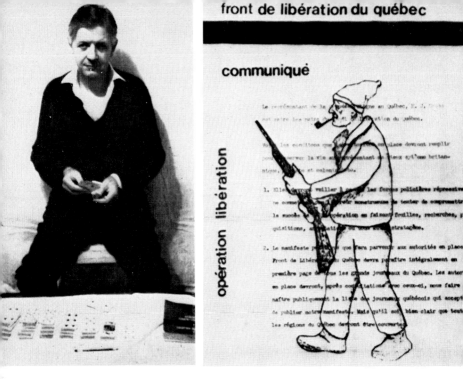

James Cross plays a game of patience while a captive of the F.L.Q.
A page from the ransom note issued by the kidnappers of James Cross.

Members of the F.L.Q. involved in the kidnapping and murder of Pierre Laporte: *(left to right)* Jacques Beaulne, Paul Rose, Francis Simard and Jacques Rose

FIVE

Terrorism As An Individual Prerogative

Modern terrorists have had less in common with historic, traditional revolutionaries than they have had with guerillas, although the three designations have been commonly used interchangeably.

Revolutionaries, historically at any rate, have been organised and disciplined resisters. Many modern nations were founded by revolutionaries. Guerillas have historically been less disciplined, less predictable, and in the view of their contemporaries, and their subsequent chroniclers, less respectable.

They very often were as troublesome in victory as in defeat, and as a general rule guerillas have found respectability unacceptable, preferring to continue to exist as advocates of gun-barrel self-expression, which, in peaceful times, is called brigandage.

Terrorists go further; they have not until recent times, called themselves terrorists, preferring — as some still prefer — to be classified as revolutionaries. But few terrorist cliques could qualify under that heading, while the more active terrorist organisations have gone beyond the limitations established by tradition, even for guerillas.

Their tactics have rarely been part of any concerted strategy toward a specific goal so much as towards pure anarchy and terror, simply in order to destroy, and this appears to arise from a cynical disbelief in any kind of successful amelioration of the conditions which have encouraged the growth of terrorism — socio-political causes. But many terrorists are not, themselves, susceptible to amelioration. In their insular world of emotional instability, retardation, immaturity, these people have derived intellectual nourishment from terrorist manuals, and, in the U.S., almost a thousand underground newspapers whose central theme has been hatred, and whose eulogies have been reserved for 'heroes of the Third World' who have murdered policemen and civil authorities, and whose exploits have included successful bombings and arson.

Twisted ideals, exaggerated and inflamed illusions of persecution and scorn, dangerous psychoses, unreasoning bitterness and hatred, genetic immaturity (which is very common among terrorists) all have had a share in the forming, as well as in the sustaining, of the amoral, incorrigible terrorist. Some of them have, like many of the Palestinian Arabs, initially embarked upon terrorism because of an ideal, but many have gone on, again like a great number of Palestinian Arabs, to become the Western or Far Eastern equivalent of the Black Septembrists — i.e., terrorists for the exclusive sake of terror.

For these people, whose mental-emotional wounds are too deep for commonplace treatment, and whose fanatical imbalance accepts an ultimate and violent death as inevitable, there will be no end to the murder and destruction until they are themselves destroyed.

These are the cadre-men of terrorism's suicide squads. They are not rare in the movement. They function as individuals or in small groups, as in Munich during the XX Olympiad, or as at the airport in Tel Aviv where only one survived, Kozo Okamoto. They are not entirely explainable. Often, they are not members of minority groups, are not among the dispossessed nor the disenfranchised, have never been persecuted nor discriminated against. Are not even poor, nor lacking in respectability.

How does one explain them? One does not, but there have always been those who have tried. The ominous element is that they have been increasing in numbers for several generations, and where it was once conceivable that such people could be confined, and were in fact confined; where, in the latter third of the twentieth century, is there an area large enough, now, to contain them all?

The man who made a fortune smuggling Pasternak's novel *Doctor Zhivago* out of the Soviet Union, Giangiacomo Feltrinelli, was never 'oppressed'. He owned a number of elaborate homes in his native Italy, was a noted raconteur, a social arbiter, a multi-millionaire jet-setter. He talked glibly and fashionably of the counter-culture and of a vague, forthcoming 'revolution', but Feltrinelli was not by most standards, even a papier-mache terrorist. He had no reason to be one.

In mid-March of 1972 someone, presumably a terrorist, perhaps an impassioned leftist wishing to influence Italy's national elections which were shortly to come, attempted to blow up a power transmission line near Milan, an act which would have caused a black-out in the nearby, sprawling city.

The explosion damaged a power structure in a field beyond Milan, but something went wrong. When the police arrived they found a badly charred corpse to which were affixed 43 unused dynamite sticks, additional bombs disguised as packets of cigarettes, and a number of false documents.

The body was that of Giangiacomo Feltrinelli, the millionaire publisher and playboy.

What reason would a man of great wealth and international prestige have for committing, or attempting to commit, such an act? The Italian rightists denounced him as a leftist terrorist, naturally, while the leftists accused him of having been a rightist attempting to simulate a leftist act of terrorism to harden Italians against leftist candidates in the forthcoming elections.

A newspaper in Turin philosophically editorialised that it was probably "useless to seek for rationality . . . in the tumultuous . . . adventures of Feltrinelli . . . He was a victim of the violence he championed and the protagonist in a romance which remains literary and unreal."

Italy's Interior Minister at the time, Mariano Rumor, assumed personal direction of the investigation, and, along with the Secret Service, made a thorough and painstaking effort to find an acceptable motive, but the best anyone could come up with was the obvious fact that Giangiacomo Feltrinelli was a terrorist. Without a valid reason, in the view of most people, certainly without any 'cause' in the accepted interpretation of that word, and without being a known associate of either the right or the left — at least the Italian authorities failed to find any such connection, and they tried to find one — Feltrinelli had inadvertently blown himself up while seeking to commit an act of terrorism. He became another enigmatic member of the brotherhood of terrorists whose motivations, at their best, have been vague, unrealistic, and by most standards of rationality, inexplicable, and which at their worst have been destruction, often pointless, and deadly.

How many of these people exist? It is indicative of the confusion among authorities in most Western nations that they rarely recognise a terrorist; generally, they still call these people 'anarchists' and make no distinction between a terrorist and a revolutionary. In the United States the F.B.I. has said that there are probably no more than 4000 hardcore dissidents in the country, while other intelligence sources claim that there are as many as 100,000 Americans who could be induced to commit violence under hardcore leadership.

But the basic number of commonplace outrages, acts of pure terrorism in the U.S., which have multiplied enormously over the past decade, suggest that there must certainly be more than 4000 nuclei, and without a doubt several times over the number of active terrorists claimed by intelligence reports.

This same conservatism can be found in most European estimates, and if the reason is to avoid frightening people, then the conservative compilers of these reports have done no one any favours.

Neither is society helped when acts of terrorism are minimised or deleted altogether from media reports, for, as Professor Stefan Passony of California's Stanford University has said, "each act of terror is a little wound to our society, and if there are enough little wounds, irreparable damage may be done".

A man such as Giangiacomo Feltrinelli cannot be swept under the rug. Nor can the small terrorist bands, called "tribes", which circulate at will through the Orient and the West, be immune to infiltration because they rarely consist of more than from three to six members, all personally acquainted with one another over long periods.

These individuals and "tribes" have learned from the guerillas, most recently Pathet Leo, Vietcong, and Cuban guerillas, that established societies are vulnerable and can be crippled by hit-and-run, infiltration tactics.

They do not expect to bring down many governments, particularly in the West, but then, by and large, they are not revolutionaries seeking to overthrow oligarchic systems in order to aid in the establishment of improved societies, they are instead simply nihilists; their effort is to cripple, maim, destroy, create dissent and confusion. In May of 1971 terrorists calling themselves 'revolutionaries' struck in Washington D.C., and through the effort called 'civil disobedience', effectively paralysed a national capital by employing guerilla tactics.

Called a 'spontaneous' demonstration, the organisers of this strike had planned it months in advance; they had detailed, printed instructions, and scale-model maps in the hands of their cadre-men, days before they sent out a call for all dissidents in the Eastern United States to rally on the Capitol. So well were the details of this assault coordinated, that guerilla-type roadblocks were set up at all major commuter routes of egress, and those who would not be intimidated into turning back, and pressed on to the federal buildings where most were employed, were again confronted; if they still persevered, they reached offices where they were very often the sole occupant.

For four days Washington was besieged by terrorists whose hit-and-run guerilla tactics were largely successful despite the best efforts of Capitol-police. Windows were smashed, cars were set afire and overturned, police were baited into well-set ambushes and savagely attacked, stores were broken into, people were beaten indiscriminately, and there was arson.

This example of 'civil disobedience' cost the city of Washington five and one-half million dollars in repair bills. The chief organisers were John Froines and Rennie Davis, admitted terrorists, both of whom were being sought by police in connection with an earlier 'spontaneous demonstration' in Chicago which had been planned to leave an impression of unprovoked police brutality, and which succeeded so well the entire nation condemned Mayor Daly's police force, and came out coast-to-coast in support of the 'peaceful demonstrators'.

The tactics of these people have been anarchic, not revolutionary. They were, themselves, not 'urban guerillas' as they have been styled, but terrorists. They have rarely promoted a 'cause', although during America's involvement in Vietnam they consistently used peace demonstrations as a cover for promoting riots and general terrorism.

If they had been revolutionaries, or guerillas seeking redress for injustices, both of whom might have been viewed with at least token sympathy, they would hardly have committed some of the depredations that to-date have best exemplified their lack of causes. For example, in October, 1970, Harvard University's Centre for International affairs, a liberal institution concerned with honest criticism of world-wide injustice, was bombed by a group calling itself the *Proud Eagle Tribe*. The damage was in excess of $40,000 dollars.

It was of course said afterwards that one terrorist group calling itself the *Proud Eagle Tribe* hardly constituted a national threat, which of course was true. And further, since the *Proud Eagle Tribe* probably consisted of no more than, at the most, ten or twenty terrorists, the 'tribe' was hardly capable of creating much widespread damage, which was also true. But, these 'tribes' are not all that rare. At least 500 of them exist in the United States, and, like the late Bader gang of West Germany, they are specialists in demolition hit-and-run warfare. They also specialise in murder, assassination, in arson, theft, intimidation, abduction and infiltration.

In New York City, in May 1971, after two policemen were critically wounded by machinegun fire in a carefully prepared ambush, a new group no one had ever heard of before, the *Black Liberation Army*, let the New York *Times* newspaper know it was responsible. In the normally quiet and orderly far north-western state of Washington, in the U.S., a recorded 1,450 attacks on policemen occurred in one year, all attributable to terrorist 'tribes'.

In California's troubled city of Santa Cruz, a lovely town in the temperate Coast Range, a Black Panther captain, Fred Bennett, was shot to death by a fellow terrorist who nearly decapitated Bennett in a burst of gunfire, then poured petrol over the corpse. It burned for 12 hours. Bennett's slaying was never officially solved, but the authorities have in fact identified his murderer. The man remains free and is still engaged in terrorist activities. There was insufficient evidence to bring him to trial.

It has rarely been true that large, established terrorist organisations have shocked the world by large-scale depredations. Even the Arab world's Popular Front for the Liberation of Palestine (P.F.L.P.) mentor of the *Fedayeen* groups, has only upon exceptional occasions undertaken anything like full-scale assaults, but has, rather, confined its participation to advice, encouragement, financial support, and guidance. Almost invariably terrorist activity has been carried out by either individuals or by small groups. The notorious Black Septembrists, most fanatical and deadly of the *Fedayeen* cadres and which has been responsible for all the recent P.F.L.P. terrorist attacks and murders — including the slaying of two U.S. diplomats in Khartoum in early 1973 — has rarely sent forth more than a dozen fanatics to perform its acts of violence.

The war of the terrorists has commonly been a conflict of individuals and small groups. Its effectiveness has been directly attributable to this fact. One man armed with a fragmentation bomb which he hurled into a Saigon restaurant, killed 40 people. One terrorist properly trained and dedicated can within moments wreck the central power facility of a large city. One knowledgeable, experienced terrorist equals a company of soldiers and a whole platoon of metropolitan police.

Multiply this knowledgeable, solitary individual by no more than five, and the results can be, and have been, appalling. Quite possibly it is this clear fact which has encouraged the FBI and other intelligence sources to conclude that there are so few nihilists in the United States. Certainly, there has never been any large-scale terrorism in the U.S., except those manipulated 'peace' or 'civil disobedience' demonstrations which have turned into bloody riots with predictable regularity almost monthly for the past ten years, and even they were usually master-minded by no more than 3 or 4 organisers.

It is also entirely possible that the U.S. authorities, like those in France, Germany, Italy and Japan, have been unable to catalogue all their resident terrorists, leaving out of consideration the constantly moving transients within the movement who pass through, coming or going, from all areas of the world, adapting to their vocation the sophisticated means of transportation which has made the world so small, and which has also made detection and detention so difficult.

Even the fact that many notorious terrorists are known to the authorities of every Western national security establishment has not really hampered the cause of terrorism very much. In West Germany subsequent to the fall of the Baader group, active terrorism declined very little. In the U.S. the restrictive surveillance exercised over the radical-violent Students for a Democratic Society (S.D.S.), and some of its more prominent chieftains such as Mark Rudd, had no inhibiting affect on the spread of U.S. terrorism.

Even among the larger militant political organisations, which have become increasingly terrorist over the past decade, but which are more properly revolutionary rather than terrorist, such as French Canada's *Front de Liberation du Quebec*, (F.L.Q.) police surveillance has minimised nothing, and in fact the F.L.Q. has become more, not less, militant, as have a number of U.S., European, and Middle Eastern terrorist and revolutionary organisations. At least some elements of these organisations have become more terrorist, but, again, these extremists, functioning individually or in small groups, have not necessarily been representative of parent organisations.

At least this has been the traditional and defensive response of some members of each parent organisation when some particular act of brutality has aroused world opinion against the entire association, as occurred when the P.F.L.P.'s Black Septembrists murdered those eleven Israeli athletes in Munich, and yet quite obviously the P.F.L.P. did not discipline the Black Septembrists, otherwise they would hardly have murdered a Belgian and two U.S. diplomats in almost the same manner less than a year later, and, in the case of the *Front de Liberation du Quebec*, all the protestations of outrage over increasingly vicious acts of terrorism, have not really minimised those acts very much, so one is almost compelled to believe the protests are window-dressing, and the acts of savagery are the F.L.O.'s actual revolutionary policy.

In any case, police surveillance notwithstanding, it has been clearly the option of the nihilist element in every organisation, whether it be revolutionary or terrorist in character, which has led to acts of barbarity. It would be seeking the impossible to expect the militant wing of revolutionary movements not to opt in favour of terrorism, at some time, and more especially in recent times when the only dissidents who have appeared to achieve popular recognition have been those who have engaged in successful terrorism.

The belief of earlier generations that these outrages could occur only in such places as Africa or the Middle East, was given a mortal blow when an act of pure terrorism occurred, in, of all places, staunchly conservative and properly law-abiding Canada, in the year 1970.

SIX

Terrorism in Canada

In the autumn of 1970, a capable and likeable British trade commissioner, James Richard Cross, 49 years of age, a native of Ireland, was abducted at gun-point from his residence on Redpath Terrace in the Mount Royal sector of Montreal, in Canada, by four members of the *Front de Liberation du Quebec* — the F.L.Q. — a separatist organisation dedicated to achieving independence for French Canda.

The question was going to be asked by a great number of people for a long time, why would the *felquistes* abduct, of all people, a British trade commissioner, rather than, perhaps, someone within Canda's own anti-separatist political establishment? And the answer, as it was subsequently given, specified the particular advantage of having as an F.L.Q. hostage someone from outside the country whose abduction would ensure an international furore, firstly, and which would, secondly, achieve maximum exposure of the F.L.Q.'s separatist aims to a, hopefully, sympathetic world.

But the F.L.Q.'s objectives were not all that crucial even in Canada, let alone the rest of the world, and by 1970 there was a very considerable extent of antagonism towards dissenters in general, and abduction in particular, not only in Europe and in Canada's southerly neighbour, the United States, but also in every sector of non-French Canada as well. Even a few outspoken non-aligned French Canadians were denunciatory. And finally, even were world opinion noticeably sympathetic, world opinion had not affected Canada's national decision-making procedures in the past, and it was therefore unrealistic to expect any such influence to affect them now. But James Richard Cross's abductors were French-Canadians, a very insular, inward people in whom calm logic and worldly awareness have never been notably endemic nor traditional, and who, although having aspired towards regional independence for generations, have acted erratically when favourable opportunities for independence have arrived, beginning back in 1775.

There has been, throughout the history of these people, a very definite capability for muffing opportunities, as well as a distorted view of the rest of the world, arising, one may presume from that very clannish inwardness which has kept them so insular for so long.

But if the abduction of 'Jasper' Cross created about as much puzzlement as apprehension, and if the *felquistes* had demonstrated small grasp of political reality in their choice of a victim, at least in their planning of the details of the abduction they did very well.

Montreal, a great urban sprawl of almost 3 million people, was more suitable as a place to hide, than one of Canada's immense forested wildernesses. While the startling news of the trade commissioner's abduction was going forth, and while Montreal's police were establishing roadblocks at every major motorway exit from the city, Cross's abductors took their blindfolded hostage on a drive through the city to Montreal North, and there, in the first floor apartment of a three-family building, where the windows had already been covered, Britain's chief trade commissioner was assigned a barren small room furnished with a mattress on the floor. Outside, the police maintained their fruitless vigil, and elsewhere Canada's leaders gradually reacted to what had happened with indignation and chagrin. Commissioner Cross was not only a guest of the Province of Quebec, in which Montreal was located, but he was also a diplomat accredited to the Canadian government. But being angry and embarrassed was not the same as being coerced.

What created the most anxiety was the conjecture that one of the more militant cells of the F.L.Q. might have abducted Commissioner Cross, and although, actually, the F.L.Q. was not generally thought to have very many, if any, genuine terrorists in it, it was known that there were fanatical bands of leftist *felquistes* who wanted an armed insurrection in Canada. These people, it was felt, were capable of committing murder.

Approximately an hour after the abduction, Canada's Prime

Minister, himself a French-Canadian, Pierre Elliott Trudeau, a flamboyant, fiftyish *bon vivant*, got the news. He had enough trouble what with antagonism increasing between Canada and the U.S. over trade. What Trudeau did not need was this kind of an embarrassment; he had been walking a political tightrope for several years, and Trudeau was enough of a pragmatist to realise that, although Canada would of course survive *l'affaire Cross*, Trudeau might not.

Immediately apparent were the options: The F.L.Q. would make demands, of course, in exchange for Commissioner Cross' safe return. Trudeau's government could accede to them — and open Pandora's box to an entire new rash of similar abductions and extortions — or it could do as Israel's Prime Minister, Golda Meir, had done during a similar, agonising travail during the XX Olympiad; stand on principal, and subsequently join in the lamentations for the slain.

The Premier of the Province of Quebec, Robert Bourassa, referring to the Latin American propensity for this sort of thing, reacted scornfully by saying the Cross affair made Canada look "like a banana republic". There were similarities, and the Cross affair was only one of them. In Montreal, Canada's largest city, roughly a year earlier, F.L.Q. militants had detonated a bomb in the financial district which injured 27 people and gutted the Stock Exchange. This was only the most recent bombing up to that time; previously F.L.Q. activists had set off hundreds of bombs, had engaged in a number of other "banana republic" acts of violence — only none of these things had been synonymous with "banana republics" in two decades.

That same day, 5th October, 1970, while Commissioner Cross was adapting to his new role as a hostage, the first note from his captors was received. It acknowledged that Cross was a prisoner of an F.L.Q. militant cell. It demanded half a million dollars, in gold, the release of 23 F.L.Q. militants then being detained by the Canadian government as law-breakers, a free flight from Canada to either Algeria or Cuba for the abductors, and concluded with some classical 'black power' rhetoric: ". . . the F.L.Q. seeks to draw world attention to the fate of French-speaking Quebecers — a majority repressed in their own territory by an economy managed for the interests of American high finance, the big racist and imperialist bosses."

Trudeau and Robert Bourassa would not accede, and subsequent to several executive sessions in Ottawa, Canada's capital, a short distance south of Montreal, as well as in the quaint city of Quebec, overlooking the busy and historic St. Lawrence River, Canada's Minister for External Affairs, Mitchell Sharp, made the formal announcement rejecting the F.L.Q.'s demands.

The F.L.Q. militants answered bluntly, stating that they would not hesitate to kill " ... J. Cross". Their deadline was 7th October, a Wednesday, but they granted a 24-hour extension, in this, as in other ways, aping the Black Septembrists of Munich almost to the letter. They also retreated from their demand for a ransom of a half million dollars in gold, and very gradually it began to appear that while Commissioner Cross was undeniably in the hands of militants, his captors were not terrorist fanatics.

The irony of the situation was that the man who would be killed by F.L.Q. terrorists, was at this time not even involved, and he was a fellow French-Canadian, and his slayers were not even in Canada, they were touring Texas in the U.S.A.

When the second deadline expired without the government acquiescing to the F.L.Q.'s demands, the militants gave Trudeau their ultimatum: unless the 23 'political prisoners' were released by 6 p.m., 10th October, no one would ever see Commissioner Cross again.

A half-hour before this ultimatum expired Quebec's Minister of Justice, Jerome Choquette, appeared on television to announce that there would be no capitulation by the government, beyond clemency if the militants gave themselves up, or safe conduct out of Canada if this was their preference, providing that Commissioner Cross was returned unharmed. Otherwise, the 23 prisoners would not be set free and no other concessions would be made by the government. "No society can expect that the decisions of its governments or courts of law can be erased by blackmail," said Choquette, "because this signifies the end of all social order."

Canada's dilemma was by this time being followed by European as well as U.S. television viewers, and shortly before Minister Choquette's announcement, which was re-broadcast as far away as Dallas, Texas, where five touring French-Canadians from Montreal, two women and three men, had been following reports of *l'affaire Cross*, a rather general and grim sense of despair had begun to prevail. It seemed that, with the possibility of their ultimatum being rejected, the *felquistes* would have no choice but to make good on their promise to kill Commissioner Cross.

Those five touring French-Canadians in Texas decided to turn about and head for home. It was the opinion of the three men, all *felquistes*, that abducting James Cross was not the way to coerce Premier Trudeau or his government. For one thing, Cross was — at least privately — very likely to be considered expendable by most Canadians. If someone had to die, then preferably it should not be a Canadian. For another thing, the death of Cross, although it would be an undeniable embarrassment to Trudeau's government, would not actually instill fear in either Premier Trudeau or his government, but, let one of *them* be endangered, and all of them would know personal fear.

While Commissioner Cross's abductors were involved in their own crisis, and both the provincial and national governments were awaiting very fearfully what must follow in the wake of Minister Choquette's pronouncement, the touring *felquistes* returned to Canada, to Montreal, and the same day Jerome Choquette made his televised pronouncement, those three *felquistes*, with another man, all members of a separate F.L.Q. cell, drove to the residence of Quebec's Minister of Labour and Immigration, burly, outspoken and shrewd Pierre Laporte, who had only a short time before defended the government's course by saying that if the extortion were acceded to ". . . the next victim could be one of us."

It was. Laporte was outside his comfortable residence on Rue Robitaille with his youthful nephew, who lived nearby, when a dark-blue car drove up. Two masked, armed men, got out, ordered Laporte into the car, and as Laporte's stunned nephew watched with Laporte's wife who had just come to the front door, the car drove away with Laporte and his abductors.

Within an hour all Canadian officials of cabinet rank had been assigned armed guards. Now, a genuine crisis existed. Every government official was justified in feeling fear. Quebec's premier, Robert Bourassa was said to be scheduled as the F.L.Q.'s next victim. Obviously, Laporte's abductors had managed in moments to accomplish what Commissioner Cross's captors had not been able to achieve in a week; Canada was in a turmoil.

The following morning Laporte's abductors made their demand. In terse, cold words they said that unless every original demand made by Cross's abductors was met within one hour, or by ten o'clock, Sunday morning, Pierre Laporte would be killed.

This time, no one was deluded, the wording of the note was altogether different, and while two separate cells of the F.L.Q. were involved, there could be little doubt but that the one holding Laporte would not temporise. An official, Claude Roquet, who examined the note from Laporte's abductors, and compared it to communications from Cross's captors, said, "Those who have Laporte — they frighten me." Roquet was not the only one they frightened, a large number of prominent Canadian citizens hired bodyguards, others did not venture out of doors, children were not allowed to leave their homes, and rather quickly Eastern Canada fell victim to a paralysis of fear.

Premier Trudeau's government had never been called upon to meet a crisis of these dimensions.

Pierre Laporte's abduction overshadowed the Cross affair, and when Laporte was allowed to send out two messages, one to his wife, the other to provincial Premier Bourassa, the latter message gave full substance to the fears — and to rumours which darkly suggested that a full-scale separitist rebellion was in the offing. Laporte wrote Bourassa not to make a vigorous police search for him, because of this were done, and the police succeeded in tracking down Laporte's abductors in their lair, "it would result in a murderous gun battle from which I would not emerge alive." Then Laporte gave the fears their most formidable support. "We are facing a well-organised escalation which can only end with the release of the political prisoners. After me there will be a third, a fourth, a twentieth. If political figures are protected they will strike at other classes of society. Act swiftly and avoid a blood bath."

Italian publisher, Giangiacomo Feltrinelli, with Sibilla Melega during
a mass demonstration in Milan, June 1967

Containing a first-aid kit and batteries, this bag was found on Feltrinelli's
body after his sabotage attempt

Police examining the body of Feltrinelli

Police surround the hotel in New Orleans in which Mark James Essex had barricaded himself. (January 1973)

Members of the *Halcones* fight students with long sticks after the student demonstration in Mexico City, June 1971

Five minutes before the 10 o'clock deadline for Laporte's execution, Premier Bourassa appealed to both of the F.L.Q. cells to contact the government so that negotiations might be undertaken. Commissioner Cross's abductors replied, naming a lawyer, Robert Lemieux, to negotiate for them, but Pierre Laporte's captors demanded immediate action on its original demands, plus two additional ones, seemingly more intent upon murder than accomodation, and to reinforce this gloomy foreboding, later the same day, well past their original deadline, they said, "This communique is the last before the execution or release of Pierre Laporte," the clear implication being that Laporte's captors were not interested in negotiating, but only in an immediate meeting of their terms, or the killing of Pierre Laporte.

There was very little hope. Fears were aroused that, should Laporte die, James Cross's murder might be triggered as a result. A Montreal psychiatrist, Dr Gustave Mort, who had been psychoanalysing apprehended F.L.Q. prisoners since 1963, was of the opinion that the F.L.Q. appealed mostly to social misfits of every kind, from those who could not adjust to society, to the simmering misfits in whom anger could turn into murderous rage without much provocation. He also felt that most of these people were not really concerned with the stated aims of the *Front de Liberation du Quebec*, were, in fact, vague about those aims. What Dr Mort was suggesting coincided perfectly with many other assessments of professional terrorists; they were alienated misfits dedicated exclusively to destruction for its own sake. These were the kind of people who now held Pierre Laporte, and, perhaps, but less likely, who also held Commissioner Cross.

The police, in the course of a quietly relentless investigation beginning only hours after James Cross had been abducted, had come up with an identity. Cross's wife Barbara tentatively identified a photograph of one of the men who had come to the house at Redpath Terrace on 5th October. His name was Jacques Lanctot. Early the previous year he had been involved in an abortive attempt to abduct the chief trade commissioner of Israel. The police were satisfied Lanctot was one of Cross's abductors. The second identity was made from a thumb-print found upon the first demand from

Pierre Laporte's abductors. It belonged to another *felquiste*, Paul Rose, a large, powerful, vicious man, a dedicated terrorist with a warped mind.

Once, detectives sighted Rose, but he escaped them, meanwhile, the crisis continued to mount. The police seemed to be helpless and the government too. Many people left the country or sent their families away. Laporte's hint of full-scale revolution, what he had called "a well-organised escalation" caused near-paralysis among Canada's businessmen and government workers. It was known, for example, that the F.L.Q. had vast stores of weapons, including bombs, and hoards of dynamite. It did nothing for the national spirit when college campuses began to echo with F.L.Q. slogans. Commissioner Cross, well into his second week of captivity, was not forgotten, but on 15th October when university students began demonstrating against Premier Trudeau's tough stand and 7,500 troops were called to Montreal, Commissioner Cross was no longer the chief actor, nor, for that matter, was Pierre Laporte. It was Trudeau.

Events came fast. Provincial Premier Bourassa told Trudeau the anticipated insurrection existed, and called upon Trudeau to invoke the War Measures Act, which no one liked because it gave almost unlimited power to the police. Trudeau was against this, but he was obliged to comply, by law, and he did. Bourassa then told Robert Lemieux, negotiator for the men holding James Cross, that the government's final offer to the *felquistes* holding both Cross and Laporte was safe delivery to Cuba, and possibly the release of five of the 23 "political prisoners" in exchange for the prompt release of both hostages.

Lemieux and other F.L.Q. members went at once to the students to denounce the government, and although professional agitators were on hand to cause trouble, the police were also out in force. There were many cries of "Vive la revolution Quebecoise", but no actual concerted riot ensued.

Now, Canadian freedom, long renowned throughout the world, was suspended. The police ruled; arrests could be made, and were made, without benefit of legal safeguards. In London it was said by a spokesman in high office that Canada was the last place in the world such a condition was expected to exist. But now the police could move directly against the F.L.Q. *Felquistes* were taken into custody in droves, even as Premier Trudeau addressed the House of Commons in these words: "I am speaking to you at a moment of grave crisis, when violent and fanatical men are attempting to destroy the unity and the freedom of Canada. Should government give in to this crude blackmail, we would be facing the breakdown of our legal system and its replacement by the law of the jungle." He also said that while there were a few times in the history of a nation when people must take a strong stand, "This is one of those times; this is one of those issues."

This same day Pierre Laporte, clearly convinced his condition was hopeless, tried to escape by holding a pillow in front of his upper body and jumping through a glass window. His captors, listening to their radio, rushed in, seized Laporte's legs and dragged him back. The following evening Premier Trudeau had his answer to the suspension of civil liberties, and to the War Act which now had Canadian police combing Montreal in an all-out search, a message from Pierre Laporte's abductors, which said, "Faced with the arrogance of the federal government and its valet Bourassa, the F.L.Q. has decided to act. Pierre Laporte was executed at 6.18 tonight." There was a map attached, directing the police to the place where Laporte's body was found in the dark-blue car in which he had been abducted one week earlier. He had been garrotted by the chain of his own religious medallion.

Commissioner James Cross learned of Laporte's murder on television. His captors, with whom he was allowed to play cards, watch television, and even argue politics, were glum, and well they might be.

It was increasingly evident that with the entire nation outraged by the Laporte murder, and with the police moving with unprecedented vigour in their manhunt, some kind of *denouément* was imminent. Also, it was now very unlikely that the abductors of James Cross could safely show themselves, or leave the city.

So they waited, and meanwhile the police located the house where Laporte had been imprisoned, and there found the fingerprints of his abductors. They were identified as Paul Rose, his brother

Jacques, Francis Simard, and a 19-year-old student radical, Bernard Lortie.

The first to be caught was Lortie, the student. He made a full confession, and eventually all of Pierre Laporte's abductors were taken into custody. Lortie and Jacques Rose were tried, convicted and sentenced to long prison terms. Francis Simard and Paul Rose, Laporte's murderers, were each imprisoned for life.

But long before these men were tried, the bizarre events leading up to the safe recovery of Commissioner Cross had begun with a very painstakingly discreet search for Jacques Lanctot, the known *felquiste* tentatively identified by Commissioner Cross's wife, Barbara, as possibly being one of her husband's abductors.

Among other things it was learned that Lanctot had a wife, Suzanne, and a baby son, Boris. It was also discovered that Suzanne Lanctot, pregnant again, never resided very long in one place, and during the course of their surveillance of Suzanne Lanctot, the police discovered that she knew a woman named Denise Quesnel, who had a daughter, Helene, both of whom were active in the F.L.Q. The police put the Quesnel woman under surveillance also, and during the last week of November, 1970, the Quesnels inadvertently led their shadows to a restaurant where they were met by one Jacques Cossette-Trudel. In the very extensive dossier which had been compiled on the James Cross abduction, there was an entry concerning a man by the name of Jacques Cossette-Trudel being married to the sister of Jacques Lanctot.

The police added Cossette-Trudel to the list of people then under surveillance. He led them to the ground floor apartment of a building on the Rue des Recollets in Montreal North where Royal Canadian Mounted Police constables established a listening post in an adjoining apartment, and eventually, after about two weeks of careful surveillance, were reasonably certain they had located the place where James Richard Cross was being held.

On 2nd December when Cossette-Trudel and a woman left the house on Rue des Recollets they were followed, and later, when they disembarked from a subway in the heart of the city, two officers moved up on each side of them and made the arrest.

After a lengthy interrogation, Cossette-Trudel admitted that

Cross was a prisoner at the house on Rue des Recollets, and that Lanctot was there with Cross. He also warned that the building was booby-trapped and at the first alarm one of Cross's captors would set off a dynamite charge.

The neighbourhood was quietly infiltrated by police and soldiers that same night — a thousand of the latter. At 2 a.m., December 3rd, the electricity into the house where Cross was being held was switched off in order to neutralise any possible electrically-operated detonation devices.

The moment the abductors discovered this, they aroused Cross, shackled him to a door and told him the police were outside. Now, for the first time in two months, James Cross was permitted to get a good look at his captors. Only one was not present: Jacques Cossette-Trudel. The others were Yves Langlois, Marc Carbonneau, and Jacques Lanctot.

Lanctot wrote a note, stuffed it into a length of pipe and threw it out into the roadway. It was then 3.20 in the morning, dark and bitterly cold. The police retrieved the pipe – with some trepidation, at first, because they thought it was a bomb – and extracted the note, which requested that a lawyer named Bernard Mergler be contacted at once and brought to the apartment building to act as intermediary between the abductors and the police for the purpose of negotiating a surrender.

This was done. As the new day dawned, and with the entire neighbourhood evacuated while soldiers and police remained in control, orders were sent out prohibiting all civilian aircraft from flying over the city, a school playground was cleared for army helicopters to land, fire trucks, ambulances and bomb squads were in position, and inside the besieged ground-floor apartment the abductors, responding to the presence of cameras, emblazoned the letters 'F.L.Q.' on the streetside windows.

Mergler was first briefed by the police, then, shortly after 11 a.m., he was taken to the apartment building, where he was admitted by Carbonneau, a squat, dark man, and Jacques Lanctot. He was introduced to Commissioner Cross. When the lawyer asked if the prisoner was well, Cross replied with a smile that he was as well as he could be, under the circumstances. Then Bernard Mergler gave the *felquistes* the government's offer: they were to be transported to the grounds of the site of the 1967 international exposition, and there James Cross would be given into the custody of an official from the Cuban consul, who had already agreed to all this. Cross was to remain with the official until Carbonneau, the Cossette-Trudels, Yves Langlois, Lanctot, along with his wife and small son — all the abductors — were safely in Havana, flown there by a Canadian aircraft.

Lanctot had doubts, but the others persuaded him to acquiesce, and a little past mid-day, the besieged apartment building was evacuated. Lanctot and Langlois made the ride to the exposition site with a six-pound dynamite bomb in their hands. Cross rode in the back seat, pale, wan and thin. Mergler rode up front with Carbonneau. At the Canadian pavilion overlooking the St Lawrence River where the world's fair had been held, William Ashford of the British Government Office, and Ricardo Escartin of the Cuban consulate, were waiting. The *felquistes* were all taken aboard a Canadian aircraft and were flown to Havana, where they landed at José Martí Airport at 1.07 a.m. the following morning, which was the signal for James Cross to be released from the technical custody of Cuban acting-consul, Ricardo Escartin. He gave a short statement to the press in which he thanked the Canadian police for their "perseverance". He also lamented the murder of Pierre Laporte by saying that "during the week when we were both prisoners, I felt closer to him than a brother."

In Ottawa, Prime Minister Pierre Elliott Trudeau, in announcing the end of the crisis, said, "I want to congratulate Mr Cross for his fortitude and his family for their great patience." He was cheered.

In early January, 1971, the troops left Montreal, and the arbitrary, nearly dictatorial police powers were phased out until, by the end of June, all civil prerogatives had been restored.

In summary, it can be noted that a country renowned for its jealously guarded civil liberties as well as its government, police and constabulary authorities, its economy to a considerable degree, its armed forces, and its entire population, were thrown into a crisis against which it really had no corrective nor defensive measures except the most harsh and arbitrary ones, by less than ten men, of which six were revolutionists and two, the actual slayers of Pierre Laporte, Francis Simard and Paul Rose, were terrorists.

Eight men against an entire country, of which only four were punished. The country lost one of its most popular administrators, the eight came through with whole skins, and are today considered triumphant heroes among French Canada's hardcore *felquistes*, who still maintain at least 150 underground revolutionary, and terrorist cells.

SEVEN

A Blueprint For Trouble

Suspension of civil liberties accompanied by arbitrary arrests and, in many cases, subsequent trials conducted by either drumhead courts martial or their civilian equivalents, have in many countries been the result of terrorism. Canada narrowly escaped the worst of these during the Laporte-Cross affair, but in some countries it has seemed that suspension of civil rights has been viewed as a preliminary step for the firm establishment of the entire sequence, and in a place such as Latin America, where democratic processes function under severe handicaps, getting the sequence reversed after a danger has passed, has not been very successful.

On the other hand, even in a country as enlightened and progressive as Canada, a reversion to near military rule, arbitrary and dictatorial, contrary in fact to the principals free people cherish, still surfaces as democracy's only response to terrorism, and that is unique. It implies two things: one — that freedom can only survive providing there is a loaded gun in the hand democracy holds behind its back, and, two — that while a number of time-tested crises have provided democracy with acceptable solutions to a great many of its problems and perils, it still has not found a better way to counteract violence than by overwhelming it with greater violence.

Perhaps, when violence and terrorism have reached such stunning proportions that everyone is personally and physically imperilled, a solution less hazardous than establishing dictatorship will be found, but until it is found, in areas such as Latin America, Africa and the East, Far and Middle, each time 'crisis rule' is established, it will not be a very simple matter, once the crisis is past, to unseat the oligarchy, the military, or the police.

The re-establishment of civil liberty in Canada could have been expected; in fact if liberty had *not* been re-established the Laporte-Cross affair would probably have seemed like a Sunday-school outing in comparison to what would have ensued. But that was Canada, not the Philippines or Uruguay.

In Latin America, terrorism has never succeeded in improving conditions, but that fact has never deterred people from becoming terrorists. Rarely have Latin American revolutions been successful in this respect, either, but, again, a small thing like idealism's failure has not prevented Latin Americans from going interminably from revolution to revolution.

Even the terribly prolonged and bloody wars waged during those chaotic times when Spain's American empire was being overthrown, when millions of courageous people responded selflessly to the *grito* of "*Independencia, Independencia!*" ultimately achieved liberation for all of Spanish America, they were not wholly successful. Latin Americans freed themselves from Spain only in order to succumb to an equal, and in many instances a worse, tyranny, from their own kind, and in the process establishing a tradition of oligarchism that found its eventual antidote in disparate varieties and degrees of liberty. But the moment national crises have arrived, the 'strongman' has invariably returned — and he has stayed.

No one is obliged to believe that democracy is the ideal form of government for all people, but many sensible people concur in the belief that without democracy, civil liberty, hope, initiative, and dignity are not even very good words.

To ensure that they are more than just words, particularly in hemispheres where oligarchy has always had many supporters, the real solution to something as sticky as terrorism must avoid the loss of civil liberty in order to overcome terror. Otherwise, in the process, they would suffer the establishment of something little better than terrorism — dictatorship.

So far, that solution has eluded lands such as Canada, the Philippine Republic, and recently-beleaguered Uruguay, the smallest South-American country, which, up until 1970, was an excellent example of both representative government at work in tumultuous and unpredictable South America, and entrenched feudalism.

It is not within the scope of this book to go a-wandering into the thickets of remedial politics — that thankless chore lying more within the purview of such prestigious and knowledgeable organisations as Britain's Institute for the Study of Conflict — but on the other hand, it cannot be expected that an American writing upon any subject will not have formed an opinion about it, whether he knows anything about the subject or not. On that basis it seems quite reasonable that the surest way to prevent terrorism and its corollary evil, dictatorship, from doing away with Latin-American liberty in particular and all liberty in general, would be for the libertarians to build into their processes of free rule preventative concepts, rather than to do as the Canadians and Uruguayans did — wait until the malignancy has benefited from Canada's and Uruguay's democratic tolerance, and has become almost inoperable, before moving to exorcise it. Because by that time it has become so big and deadly that it can only be done away with by the most drastic surgery — and everyone suffers then.

Uruguay, a country of roughly 3½ million people (bordered by Latin America's two most powerful nations, Brazil and Argentina) has long been a particular target of Latin America's *fidelistas*, communist Cubans, both because it is weak — its army is less than 15,000 strong and has not fought in well over a half-century — and because although both Brazil and Argentina have more or less stamped out their own communist malignancies, if *fidelistas* could triumph in Uruguay — as the *fedayeen* tried to do in Jordan — they would have a haven of immunity, in theory anyway, from which to export communism to both of Uruguay's adjacent, richer nations.

Montevideo, Uruguay's largest and most cosmopolitan city, with a population of 1½ million, well over one-third of the country's population, is, like most Latin American metropolises, a study in contrasts between the very wealthy and the very poor. It has for generations been the spawning ground for every kind of aggressive activist from revolutionaries and urban guerillas to outright terrorists. Because of its location on the River de la Plata, adjacent to the Atlantic Ocean, it has historically been a sanctuary for smugglers and pirates, and its past has been lawless enough, and colourful enough, to allow the oldtime tolerances to linger. Also, Montevideo is sufficiently cosmopolitan and sophisticated not to make an issue of the illegalities which most of the wealthy and powerful people have not usually been affected by, and which the very poor quite often benefit from.

In fact, the entire country, caught up in a disastrous dream of run-away socialism over the past few decades, did not really make any very concerted attempt to stop the growth of a terroristic and revolutionary underground which grew immensely. This was largely because Uruguay's variety of democracy, like that of Canada, had no built-in safeguards against that sort of thing.

Further, lest those who are forever denouncing the military forget it, the civilian establishments of democracy have invariably been equally as blind, corrupt, and inexcusably stupid, and perhaps, because they are larger and commonly more powerful, they have also been more self-centred and more phlegmatically indolent. In Uruguay, this was particularly true, for even after there was ample reason to be alarmed over the growing power and the outrageous savagery of the terroristic underground, the Tupamaro movement, nothing was really done to destroy it. Many of the ambitiously self-serving politicians, uncertain as to just how powerful the Tupamaros were, how many votes they might control, even encouraged them, tactfully and warily, but still encouraged them.

Gradually, from a humble beginning, the terroristic revolutionary Tupamaro movement grew between the year it was founded by Raul Sendic (a leftist one-time law student) in 1962, until it had its fatal confrontation with the government of Uruguay in 1972, from a handful of disenchanted, idealistic youthful revolutionaries and completely *un*idealistic murderous, misfit terrorists, until, in a country of $3\frac{1}{2}$ million people, its numbers were variously estimated at from 100,000 to 300,000. It became, without a question, the best example of organised terrorism in the Americas, a model even the Cubans could extol and envy.

Obviously, in order for such an organisation to flourish and prosper with such unprecedented rapidity, and to gain such strength and numbers within so short a period of time, there had to be very excellent reasons.

Uruguayan 'democracy' was the reason. Not simply the lack of preventative safeguards, although those undeniably encouraged the practically unimpeded growth of the Tupamaro movement, but the kind of 'democracy' which had, over the years, seen the vested entrenchment of roughly 2,500 people, who controlled the businesses, the land, the politics and the economy of Uruguay, a variety of feudalism which has been predominant — not *only* in Latin America, but in this case has been particularly predominant there — for many generations.

No one has to disapprove of this, or any other kind, of democracy, or approve of it either, but the fundamental fact supporting the inevitability of the changes which are definitely coming, is based on the plain fact that wealth has not been as synonymous with power for the past twenty years, as numbers have been. In other words, 2,500 Uruguayan millionaires, probably unknowingly, were approaching a confrontation with 50,000 destitute or disenchanted dissidents in 1965, 70,000 in 1968, 100,000 in 1970, 200,000 in 1971, and so on. Their wealth was not enough in 1965; by 1971 there was no question at all about the wealth of the few equalling the sheer power of numbers of the many.

Thus it was possible for the Tupamaro movement to flourish with unprecedented power and growth. But that was not the only reason. Another was Uruguay's economy. For many years Uruguay prospered primarily from its agriculture — its meat, hide and wool exports — and at the apex of the good years there was little real destitution; during those years the Tupamaros could not have gained a toehold. But Uruguay's year-in-year-out prosperity in the early and mid-years of the present century encouraged a sense of security that took no cognizance of the possibility that life in Uruguay, or elsewhere for that matter, was not an ever-blooming economic rose garden.

Uruguay experimented with a number of commendable social programmes. Commendable because they were enlightened and progressive, but only in a country which did not carry all its economic eggs in one basket, and which had a large financial reserve, which Uruguay did not have. Uruguay inaugurated an eight-hour workday at a time when such a thing was almost unheard of in Latin America. It undertook brave programmes of free education, unemployment insurance, workmen's compensation and retirement pensions. Uruguayans became an educated, liberal-minded, insularly protected and secure people; then, not long after the Second World War, — which had given impetus to the development of such things as synthetic rubber and wool — meat prices fell and Uruguay, along with other nations, faced an inevitable loss of income, but by then Uruguayans had grown very comfortable with their hot-house variety of national paternalism, and even had national leaders dared suggest it could not continue, no one would have believed them.

A Uruguayan could retire at about 50 years of age on a pension that was the same as his salary or wages had been. A woman who had a child and who had worked at least ten years, could also retire on a pension. Uruguay's workforce of one million was required to support a retired segment of the national population which numbered almost 500,000 people as late as 1972. And if this was not sufficiently disastrous, inflation, which had been troubling all Latin America (as well as North America) since the end of the Second World War, took an enormous bite out of everyone's pay or pension packet. This guaranteed, among other things, that the educated Uruguayans, trained as euphoric liberals, became baffled, at first, then angry, and finally, because they were unable to appreciate the fact that there really was no such thing as an ever-blooming economic rose garden, they began the witch hunt which, in Latin America, has traditionally ended at the doorway of that malevolent old Croesus of the north, the United States.

Somehow or other 'Yankee imperialism' was to blame, and the way to combat that, clearly, was to join the brotherhood of the bearded ones — Cuba's inspired and heroic *Barbudos* — also known as *Fidelistas*. This then, brought Uruguay to its final reason for having such a phenomenally successful underground movement.

Cuba, which had been exporting revolution and terrorism since shortly after Fidel Castro came to power, functioning in this regard as a hemispherical military command post, already had guerillas engaged in hit-and-run combat in the Argentine, and had, until shortly before Cuban support of the Uruguayan Tupamaro movement, been an active participant in similar operations inside the borders of Uruguay's other neighbour, Brazil.

The Brazilians, at times a no-nonsense pragmatic people, had quite effectively eliminated their *Fidelistas*, but in Argentina the skirmish continued, and in fact still continues. Uruguay, then, suffering from its economic imbalance, and with its own embryonic, angry underground movement in the making, presented the *Fidelistas* a golden opportunity. Nor were they slow about seizing it.

There was, however, one unique difference between the traditional Latin-American revolutionary counter-culture as promoted by the Cubans, and what evolved in Uruguay. Almost without exception, earlier South American insurrectionists had not only come from the countryside, themselves, but they had functioned there, taking advantage of jungles, forests, enormous stretches of overgrown and uninhabited countryside in order to successfully press their guerilla wars. In Uruguay, Montevideo was the key to the country. Hit-and-run strikes in the hinterland could not really be expected to injure the country, or endanger the government, very much.

The 'heroes' of international revolution had started their march to power in the backlands. Castro, Mao Tse-tung, among others had drawn from the metropolitan areas, they had not started there. In Uruguay, Raul Sendic's movement began in the metropolitan centre, Montevideo. His Tupamaro movement never really worried much about the countryside; it did not have to. Power in Uruguay was not in the countryside; even recruitment from the hinterlands was unnecessary.

Sendic's Cuban allies and supporters learned lessons from their Tupamaro co-conspirators not only about urban warfare, but also how a metropolis could, literally, become two cities, one above ground, one below ground. What the Tupamaros built would have fascinated Tolkien, all science-fiction writers who had been imagining such a fantastic situation for years.

The difference was that Tolkien imagined it, and the Tupamaros actually did it.

EIGHT

Tupamaro Terrorism

The Tupamaros adapted their name from an 18th-century folk-hero, Tupac Amaru, an alleged inca (emperor) who was put to death by the Spaniards for leading an unsuccessful uprising against them. The founder of the Tupamaros, Raul Sendic Antonaccio, as erratic and unstable as he may have been in other ways, shared with other Tupamaro leaders a unique penchant for organisation. It was this capability which enabled the movement, more properly known as the National Liberation Movement, or M.L.N., to function so well from the beginning. Although, generally, the contemporary conviction among international terrorists and revolutionaries supported the idea that cells within a movement should not know very much about other cells, or even other individuals in the movement, this seldom existed among the Tupamaros. In fact, as time passed and the movement grew strong enough to challenge Uruguay's government, the M.L.N. began to appear less as an underground movement and more as a militant, political party.

The M.L.N. had an executive committee of five, and a competent secretariat of seven. The five formulated policies at the top, giving orders to the secretariat, who passed down the orders to the 'columns', or fieldgroups, which were in size equal at the least to a company of soldiers, and which were quite often nearer battalion size. The columns were numbered; they were usually led, or officered by experienced and proved commanders. The columns were the M.L.N.'s 'soldiers'. In their ranks were a variety of individuals ranging all the way from students, felons, disaffected soldiers and bureaucrats, to businessmen, lawyers, doctors, and politicians. There was, right from the start, a weighty percentage of social misfits, genuine terrorists. Raul Sendic's immediate associates at the outset were educated, embittered idealists, always young, either in their teens or twenties and often from upper middle-class families. Generally, these and other Tupamaros parroted the time-worn leftist rhetoric about creating the ideal socialist state, but genuine objectives, and even specific details, were lacking. The fundamental purpose of these people was not actually to establish anything, but instead it was to destroy existing social structures. As with all terrorists, there was plenty of cooperative, cohesive effort towards destruction, and almost no responsible, detailed objectives serving as an ultimate goal beyond the stage of destruction. As the movement gained momentum, it increasingly functioned like an army of brigands, far closer to the tradition of the Mafia than of any genuine revolutionary movement, even though there were without question, many genuine socially-oriented revolutionaries within its ranks.

Cuba, of course, sent seasoned guerillas to guide, observe, and support the Tupamaros. Chile's president, Salvador Allende, a rare individual in the leftist world, a popular leader freely elected to a national presidency, likewise recognised the Tupamaro insurgency as America's most powerful and successful underground movement, and not only lent active support, but made Chile a sanctuary, as well as a diplomatically immune staging area, for Uruguay's underground.

The movement attracted a great number of Uruguay's educated graduates who came forth from academe armed with the credentials which entitled them to a rightful place of authority and prestige in a paradise which did not exist. While a few worthwhile Uruguayan students accepted this blow, adjusting to it by donning a tin beak and getting down to scratch in the real world with real people, others vented their ire against a society *which was*, by joining the M.L.N., and seeking through terror-tantrums, not to create a society which should have been, but to destroy a system which had not been able, for many reasons, – including a geographical one – to live up to their unrealistic expectations. These became, by and large, the nihilists, the destroyers – the genuine terrorists.

It was these educated, but not necessarily mature, individuals, who gave the movement its ultimate sophistication. They were adequately erudite to edit the newspapers, to compile the chronicles, and to write the virulent propaganda. They made the Tupamaro movement the world's most formidable guerilla organisation. They, and others, implemented the campaigns of terror against all organised authority. They were also the ones who devised clever schemes to intimidate government officials at all levels, and through the use of sardonic humour, they made a number of Uruguay officials appear ludicrous. To encourage empathy they punctured the pomposity of a number of overbearing and conceited politicians, and while the common people were amused, the Tupamaros also organised and activated squads of assassins.

The movement's leadership employed an ingenuity, a virtuosity, that guaranteed success. Membership increased, and along with it, Tupamaro power and sophistication kept pace. A photographic establishment, fully staffed with professionals, turned out bogus documents by the ream, auto-repair and alteration garages were set-up to modify or armour stolen cars. There were even three furniture manufacturing facilities created, whose speciality was the construction of items in which arms, papers, and even people, could be secreted. A clothing establishment made exact duplications of armed service and police uniforms for one individual or for many individuals.

By the time the M.L.N. was engaged in outright conflict with the Uruguayan government, it had Montevideo, and the countryside beyond, honeycombed with cells and 'columns'. Abduction squads moved at will against those in authority who were considered the movements most formidable foemen. These squads also struck at foreigners. They not only abducted the British Ambassador, Sir Geoffrey Jackson, and held him for eight months in one of their *berrentines*, or underground prisons, but they also took a 65-year-old American agronomist, Claude Fly, held him seven months, and only released him when a near-fatal heart attack almost killed him. They abducted Dias Gomide, the Brazilian consul; altogether the Tupamaros abducted close to twenty foreigners, nearly all possessing diplomatic status.

They established broadcasting stations, even their own hospitals in the labyrinthine underground beneath Montevideo, completely staffed and equipped. When the police moved, eventually, in concerted force, it was too late because the M.L.N. had more execution squads than the police had field units. Generally, assassinations took place on Friday. Uruguayans dreaded what commonly took place on this day. Killing policemen became commonplace; many police and judicial figures became so frightened that when Tupamaros were rumoured to be on the move, they would not venture out, or, when Tupamaros were apprehended and brought to trial, judges would not sentence them, would order them released from custody.

Uruguay became a haven for terrorists. They arrived from the West Indies, Cuba, throughout Latin America, Europe, and the U.S. The M.L.N. functioned practically at will, and the $100,000 a month which it was estimated was required to finance its endeavours, was to a considerable extent taken at gunpoint from banks and business establishments. Other funding arrived in the form of grants from leftist fronts beyond Uruguay's borders.

By 1970 the Tupamaros had become an inspiration to dissidents all over the world. Their organisational efficiency was a model for such groups as the Provisional Wing of the Irish Republican Army.

Other terrorist and revolutionary organisations had tried to take over nations; this was a prime objective, always, as when the Palestinians, supported by Syrian armour and Soviet financial and technical assistance, had attempted to conquer Jordan, but none had succeeded. The Tupamaros were definitely moving towards that goal by 1970, and they were doing it in a manner which certainly appeared to guarantee success.

Bombing was of course, commonplace, as were arson, murder, intimidation and blackmail. Repeated declarations of crises by the Uruguayan government changed nothing; the Tupamaros, by intimidation in high places, by cajolery at the *campesino* level, tightened their grip on the country. Outside aid gave added impetus, as did outside technical assistance. For example, the underground burrowing which exemplified the Vietcong's ability to vanish in the face of American advances during the recent Vietnam conflict, was adapted to the Uruguayan situation. In Montevideo not only were underground sewer complexes utilised, but additional tunnelling helped create an amazing complex of prisons, hospitals, command posts, even rest areas. There was a city beneath a city. The M.L.N. improved upon this 'middle kingdom' concept so well that underground corridors even went beneath prison walls, and under government armouries.

The M.L.N. rented villas, burrowed beneath them in all directions, linking their above-ground facilities with a maze of underground ones. Excavated earth was secretly taken away at night. Tupamaro ingenuity was demonstrated many times. An example would be the time the Uruguayan authorities, offering evidence of *their* ingenuity, located an apartment where two prominent Tupamaros resided, and arrested both terrorists. Then, instead of departing with their prisoners, the police remained at the apartment. Each time a Tupamaro came calling, he was bagged. It was a successful haul; among the nine prominent Tupamaros captured, was the notorious and elusive founder of the M.L.N., Raul Sendic.

Very early in the morning of 7th September, 1971, about two months later, the Tupamaros took their turn. Previously, the night before, Tupamaro tunnellers and guerillas invaded a home opposite the Punta Carretas Prison, and while the household's rightful occupants watched the floor was ripped up. Several hours before dawn men began coming up out of the ground into the house! Including Raul Sendic, 106 Tupamaros emerged by way of a 120-foot tunnel which had taken two months to excavate, and which ran under the prison walls, across the street, beneath the occupied house, and ended at the hole in the floor!

The M.L.N. often kept its hostages in underground holes. The one where the American soils expert, Claude Fly, was first incarcerated, was, according to Fly, "about three feet deep, and I had to bend over to crawl to a blanket-covered cot in one corner . . . my kidnappers clamped a lid over the hole and left me to meditate on my fate in darkness and terror." Subsequently, when the Brazilian consul, Dias Gomide, was abducted, he spent some time in another cell, this one 4 by 6½ feet, made of lumber and wire mesh, in which Claude Fly had also been imprisoned during his 208-

day captivity. The British ambassador spent even more time in the *berrentines*; he was an M.L.N. hostage for eight months, never knowing from day to day when he would get a bullet through the head.

Meanwhile, above ground, Tupamaro expertise in all avenues of guerilla conflict had brought on the final crises. Uruguayan President Jorge Pacheo Arec, like Canada's Pierre Elliot Trudeau and Israel's Golda Meir, would not succumb to the M.L.N.'s blackmail. He would not discuss a release of hostages based upon M.L.N. demands, which would have virtually given national sovereignty into the hands of the terrorists. To bring pressure upon the obdurate Chief Executive, from the U.S., which supported Uruguay's legitimate government, another American on loan to Uruguay, was killed. In late July 1971, a former police chief of Richmond, Indiana, who was in Uruguay as an employee of the U.S. Agency for International Development, Dan Mitrione, was on his way to the U.S. Embassy in Montevideo, when a truck rammed the car he was riding in, and before the former police chief could recover, Tupamaros ran up and began beating him. Mitrione was also shot in the chest. Then he was abducted and the government was notified that unless 150 Tupamaros were freed from custody, Dan Mitrione would be killed. The government refused. A short while later Mitrione's corpse was found in an abandoned car. He had been shot in the head.

Claude Fly was abducted shortly after the Mitrione affair had been concluded. The British Ambassador Geoffrey Jackson was next. He was taken in the identical manner Dan Mitrione had been captured; his car was rammed and Ambassador Jackson was hauled off in a second car.

The rash of abductions, plus the Mitrione murder, lent substance to a growing conviction that the M.L.N. was going to inaugurate a wholesale bloodbath of its captives. This feeling was rampant not only in Uruguay, where the embattled government, police, and armed services, had their backs to the wall, but elsewhere as well. Britain, the U.S., and a number of other countries, many of them neighbouring Latin American nations, condemned what was happening in Uruguay, and watched events with grave misgivings.

Then, as 1971 drew to a close, there was a lull. The M.L.N., confident it had strong support, through sympathy or fear, prepared to meet the challenge when President Pacheco's term as Uruguay's Chief Executive expired. It organized a coalition called a 'Broad Front' which included all leftists, communists, socialists, and every other variety of political aberrationist, along with the terrorists, and undertook a vigorous campaign to win popular support. Its leaders and strategists had reason to believe they could triumph *via* the ballet box; besides the unquestionable terroristic power they had, Uruguay's economic situation had steadily worsened, largely as a result of Tupamaro activity. There was even less promise of economic recovery by the end of 1971 than there had been before. Uruguay was in a very poor way, economically, socially, and politically.

The previous year, in Chile, where a similar disenchantment with national conditions had driven embittered people to experiment with communism, the Marxist Salvador Allende had been elected president.

The M.L.N. halted its terrorism — which was probably all that saved many of its hostages from being executed — and announced that it would seek power through legitimate channels. Then, probably to influence the waverers, it also announced that if the Tupamaros did not win the election, the M.L.N. would inaugurate a new reign of terror with a view towards bringing on a full-scale revolution.

Presidential aspirant, Juan Maria Bordaberry, a rancher and a conservative, who was not well-known but who was clearly anti-M.L.N. was the clear choice of those who opposed the Tupamaros.

For a while, as long as the electioneering was in progress, there was relative peace in Uruguay. On election day the country was like a graveyard. Then the results were announced. Juan Bordaberry had been elected President of Uruguay by a 90-percent vote! The M.L.N. had polled only 18.3 percent of the popular vote.

At once the M.L.N. prepared a list of victims for its squads of assassins. On 14th April, Tupamaro terrorists ambushed four government and police officials, beginning at 7 a.m., and killed all four without warning. The nation was shocked and outraged. The balance of that day was spent in gunfights in the streets between M.L.N. columns, police, and the Uruguayan army.

The final crisis, exactly as promised by the M.L.N. had come. Uruguay's Congress, like Canada's Parliament, suspended civil liberties, declared that a state of internal war existed, and gave power into the hands of the police and the army. Defence Minister Enrique Magnani said, "We are at war!" but these broad powers of suppression had been used before against the M.L.N. without very much success, and one of the men assassinated on 14th April, Acosta y Lara, former Under Secretary of the Interior, once offered a fair summary of the situation when he said, "Blood will flow in our country for a long time to come, because the guerillas cannot win power by revolution, and we, the majority of Uruguayans who support democracy, will not give up the battle any more than the Tupamaros will."

Nevertheless, the 14th April assassinations were a mistake. Uruguayans who had never cooperated with the police, out of fear, freely cooperated with the army, and many people who had been at least luke-warm towards the M.L.N. up until this time, turned against it after the assassinations and the gunfights in the streets.

Congress enacted stringent new laws which gave the military courts sufficient power to sentence proven Tupamaros to terms as long as 30 years in prison. And those were the lucky ones; soldiers did not bring to trial many Tupamaros taken in arms.

Legal rights were abrogated, along with civil rights, informers turned up in droves. Raul Sendic was shot down and wounded, in a battle with government supporters; three other members of the M.L.N.'s supreme executive committee, Fernandez Huidobro, Alberto Candian Grajales and Marenales Saenz, were killed.

Of the secretariat, one was killed, four were taken into custody and two fled, probably to either Cuba or Chile. Column commanders were killed in battles and otherwise, while some were taken into custody, and those of their followers who chose to fight it out were decimated, those who chose a more prudent course either yielded peaceably, dropped from sight, or became collaborators. Of the nearly 200 Tupamaros who had escaped from confinement, more than 150 were re-arrested.

The government's grim sweep did not let up. Underground arms caches were captured, much stolen hospital equipment, cars, broadcasting equipment, and printing presses were located and confiscated.

The original suspension of civil rights granted by Congress for 30 days at the beginning of the crisis was extended on 30th June for an additional 90 days. By the end of that time the M.L.N. had been rather thoroughly defeated. Nevertheless the emergency powers were again extended, near the end of September, for another 60 days, even though the M.L.N. as a national threat no longer existed, although there were still many M.L.N. leaders at large, and many Tupamaro 'soldiers' at liberty.

Uruguay, as a historic welfare-democracy, could very well revert to its former status as a land of civil liberties, and the late Acosta y Lara may have been incorrect in his assessments concerning the duration of the trouble in Uruguay, now that the Tupamaros have been sent helter-skelter in disarray, but it would be well to bear in mind that the social and economic ills which allowed a thing like the M.L.N. to be conceived in the first place, remain endemic in Uruguay. It would also be well to bear in mind that the terrorists, the executioners, those who were never really dedicated to establishing a Castro-like dictatorship in Uruguay, which was the goal of the genuine revolutionists, were not eliminated, they were simply scattered to Chile, Cuba and other countries, and without much doubt a great number of them never left Uruguay.

Economic and social ills have invariably triggered such people. Not because they have had either solutions, nor even any genuine belief that solutions existed, but simply because society's shortcomings have provided them, not with the reason — they have never needed reasons — but with the excuse to embark upon campaigns of terror, their objectives being destruction for destruction's sake.

Smashing the leadership of an organisation such as the M.L.N. may deprive the killers of their protective umbrella, but it has never eliminated the genuine terrorists.

NINE

Augmenting the Dilemma

Israel's armed forces chief of staff reported in early 1973 that since the slaying in Munich the previous September of eleven Israeli Olympic athletes, his nation had attacked 33 terrorist bases in Syria and Lebanon, killing or wounding 1,000 people. This was in accordance with Prime Minister Golda Meir's announcement that Israel would "smite the terrorists wherever and whenever we can find them".

But, obviously, air strikes and commando raids have not proved a deterrent. Even in Israel there has been a widespread feeling that retaliation is not the answer. A senior Israeli military officer implied the general feeling of futility when he said, "I don't know any answer to Munich . . . unless you kill every terrorist that had something remotely to do with it. That means military leaders who were behind them, and countries that were behind them, etc." Another veteran of Israel's army said, "I know of no one single way of wiping out terrorism. There must be a combination of ways."

Developing methods for the mitigation of terrorism are certainly not beyond the capability of most national leaders, or their advisers, but at least in Israel there has been a rather steadfast refusal to move in this direction, preferring instead to adopt the posture of Maccabean obstinacy. This has, quite clearly, guaranteed the continuation of terrorist activity against Israel and its people, at home and abroad. It has also gone far towards creating enemies of the state of Israel, even among people who have been Israel's supporters and sympathisers, not only in Europe and America, but even in the Arab world.

An example which is neither a rare nor exclusive one, can be found in the plight of the Christian Arabs of two rural villages, Ikrit and Berem, near Israel's border with Lebanon. These people, who have traditionally been farmers, were rarely molested by other Arabs, who were commonly Mohammedans, and yet the people of Ikrit and Berem, being 'different', being Christian Arabs in the world of Mohammedan Arabs, could readily identify with the Israelis, who were also 'different', and when the upheaval of 1948 occurred, which culminated in independence for the state of Israel, the villagers of Ikrit and Berem, who were friendly towards, and in sympathy with, the Israelis, did not abandon their homes as did most other border Arabs. They had been assured that the Israelis came as friends and liberators.

Eventually, when the conflict became increasingly fierce, the Christian Arabs of Ikrit and Berem were asked to leave their villages and farms "for fifteen days" by the government of Israel, so that they would not become inadvertent victims of the fighting.

They left, seeking shelter in other villages which were beyond the war's perimeter. That was in 1948, twenty-seven years ago. They were never invited back, and despite innumerable appeals for justice to the Israeli government, were not allowed to return, despite the fact that these Christian Arabs have never been accused by Israel of hostility, have in fact been recognised as supporters of the new state — which, from its beginning pledged equal treatment, without discrimination against, all Israeli citizens — and, during the long years of waiting, many of the men of Ikrit and Berem served honourably and courageously in Israel's armed forces.

Finally, in late August of 1973, after almost a full generation of waiting, appealing, and praying, the Christian Arabs of Ikrit and Berem sought to 'go home'. The Israelis met them with guns, arrested fourteen of their leaders as invaders and scattered the others. Israel refused to honour the 1948 pledge and rejected the latest plea of the homeless and destitute villagers of Ikrit and Berem on the grounds that, as Arabs by descent, who may have been tainted through their quarter-century odyssey among other Arabs — who possibly were hostile to Israel — the Christian Arabs were undesirables.

There were other reasons, and at least one of them had nothing at all to do with idealism: much of the land once farmed by the people of Ikrit and Berem was now the property of Israeli farmers. Most of what had been left behind in the towns had been appropriated by Jews.

Israel's Attorney General, Meir Shamgar, reiterated the government's stand with respect of the possibility of contamination, in the face of the more immediate issue of indemnification and repatriation. To Israel's officials the people of Ikrit and Berem were outcasts — even though, at the very time this was Israel's official policy, the Christian Arabs were defending Israel in the Israeli armed forces.

When Archbishop Yussef Raya, spokesman of the Greek Catholic minority of Israel met with Prime Minister Meir, and she refused repatriation and indemnification, the Archbishop said, "There is neither democracy or liberty" in Israel, and there was "not enough justice" either.

Additionally, when some of Israel's outstanding intellectuals challenged the government's stand on the issue of the people of Ikrit and Berem, Prime Minister Meir called their attitude an "erosion" of Zionist faith.

All this, notwithstanding the demonstrable fact that these Christian Arabs were never the fair-weather variety of friends and allies Israel has so consistently encountered throughout her hectic and tumultuous struggle for survival. The people of Ikrit and Berem have steadfastly refused to be identified with pan-Arab groups such as *Al Fatah* or the Popular Front for the Liberation of Palestine (P.F.L.P.). Despite all that has befallen them, they continued to voice a belief in ultimate justice — even when, in 1952, the Israeli army systematically dynamited their villages to prevent them from being used by hostile Arab guerrillas operating out of Lebanon, and no subsequent offer of indemnification was made.

A quarter of a century of constancy repaid by a quarter of a century of betrayal. For Israel's most fanatical foes, the Palestinian Arabs, less then a third of that length of time was required to turn them into Israel's most bloody and implacable adversaries; how much longer will it be before the people of Ikrit and Berem accept the fact that the Israelis have no intention of offering them justice?

How long before they, too, become still another faction dedicated, not to the overthrow of the Israeli government, but become, like the Palestinians, totally dedicated to the complete subjugation of the nation of Israel?

Recently it was written that the search for a way to prevent terrorism against Israel and Israelis "has been under way in the military planning rooms and the councils of Israel" for many months, and yet, as in the instance of the Christian Arabs of Ikrit and Berem, one is entitled to wonder whether any solution to this augmentation of the dilemma can possibly come out of a 'military planning room' where the mace bearers of Israel do not deal in justice, but deal rather in force and retaliatory violence, things which exacerbate rather than ameliorate or arrest the doubts and suspicions of a nation such as Israel, which has already presented her adversaries with sound reason for mistrust.

Nor have the preponderantly hostile Arabs of the Middle East failed to add the plight of the villagers of Ikrit and Berem to their propaganda base, an opportunity which has further strengthened Arab resolve, and which has also, for Israel, compounded the dilemma of terrorism.

Arab propagandists could truthfully emphasise the fact that despite Israel's contention that the people of Ikrit and Berem could be security risks, there is no real evidence of this at all. On the contrary, the Christian Arabs have been infinitely more loyal to Israel than many Israelis have been. Also, Arabs in Israel constitute no more than 13 percent of the national population, and Christian Arabs constitute no more than 20 percent of the 13 percent. As security risks the entire Ikrit-Berem group could not be as dangerous to Israel, unless recruited by the Palestinians as terrorists against Israel, as, for example, one Jew named Israel Beer who, while serving on Israel's General Staff, and as an intimate of the patriarch, David Ben Gurion was a Soviet intelligence agent who provided Israel's most powerful enemy with minute details of Israeli and U.S. secrets.

Israel has, through other instances which parallel the case of the Ikrit-Berem villagers, alienated powerful and influential Arabs who were not, in the past, altogether antagonistic to the idea of a Jewish state in the Middle East.

It has been one thing to betray a handful of homeless people who could not, without leadership and funds, pose much of a threat, especially since their situation was hardly known outside of Palestine, but it was something quite different when Israel alienated Arabs of position, wealth and power, through an identical tactlessness.

During the 1967 war, which ended so ignominiously for the Arabs, when Israel occupied Syria's Golan Heights, an influential Druse leader, Sheik Kamal Kanj, a former member of the Syrian Parliament, was outspokenly favourable toward the invaders. Kanj seemed wary of Soviet penetration of the Middle East, most particularly Syria. Israel, supported by the U.S., appeared the lesser of two evils, and in any event Israel's intention seemed not to extend beyond securing its own borders, even though this meant pushing those borders beyond the 1948 limits. Israel did not propose to conquer Syria, but by 1967 it seemed quite clear that the U.S.S.R., with growing interest and impetus, could quite conceivably have something more ominous in mind than simply supplying Syria with armaments and technical advisers.

A man as well-informed as Kamal Kanj had ample opportunity to observe how Soviet aid in other lands had culminated in Soviet domination. A few men like Sheik Kamal Kanj in any country, were the best of all assurances that sovietization did not occur.

At his villa in the village of Majdal Shans, Kamal Kanj entertained Israel's Defence Minister, Moshe Dayan. He also had as his houseguest upon another occasion, Yigal Allon, Israel's Deputy Premier. Kanj sought to promote amicable relations between Syria and Israel — a next to impossible undertaking in the face of Israel's refusal to relinquish the strategic Golan Heights — but the Druse leader was neither a novice nor an optimist; if he thought a possibility existed, it existed.

For the Israelis, Kamal Kanj, a person of power among Israel's roughly 35,000 Druse, was a worthwhile political ally. His brother was military commander of the Damascus area, and Kanj himself was on friendly terms with many Syrians of influence. This was not the kind of a man for the Israelis to antagonise.

His friendship for the new owners of the Golan Heights did not increase his popularity among either the nationalist of leftist

Syrians, and eventually Sheik Kamal Kanj was arraigned *in absentia* by a Syrian court and sentenced to 18-months imprisonment for collaborating with the Israelis.

He remained a friend of Israel. Then, between pressure from Damascus, and an attitude towards him among highly-placed Israelis of indifference and neglect, almost of contempt, Sheik Kamal Kanj began to change, and by early 1971, he was in contact with both nationalist Syrians and hostile West-Bank Arabs. The most valuable ally Israel had in Syria had been alienated; a man whose cultivation and continued friendship was more vital to the Israelis than a battalion of armour, was no longer willing to labour towards either a compromise nor a *detente*, and in fact, having made the transition, having announced his return to the role of a leader among anti-Israel Arabs by saying that "We Druse are an inseparable part of the Arab nation," Sheik Kamal Kanj sought reinstatement among the Syrians by collecting military information about the Israelis for his government.

He may have been detected at this by the Israeli intelligence service, which has been consistently one of the best in the world, and if so, it is possible that Kanj's telephone calls were monitored. He carried on a rather extensive communication with both the West Bank and Damascus. In any event, in May, 1971, an armed party of Israelis arrived outside Kamal Kanj's residence, surrounded it, took Kanj into custody, along with a Syrian non-commissioned officer who was visiting the villa, and spirited the Druse leader off to captivity on a charge of spying for Syria.

The inevitable result of this was a furore among the Syrians, but more specifically, among the Druse over whom Kamal Kanj had exerted a restricting influence, and the predictable aftermath was a violent oath of retaliation, ensuring more terrorism against Israel, not only from outside the country, but also from within Israel.

Provocations which result in either new or increased terrorism are certainly not confined to the Middle East, but because that area is and has been for a long while probably more actively troubled by terrorists than most other areas, it has offered excellent examples on how terrorism, rather than being mitigated, has been encouraged. The current popular view is oriented in that direction; people have been reading of Palestinian terrorism so consistently that they are accustomed to it in that area, and undoubtedly the retaliation which inevitably follows in its wake is also expected. But it can be reasonably doubted that many observers who see, firstly, the terrorism, then, secondly, the retaliation, appreciate that while the acts of terror ensure retaliation, the same applies in reverse; acts of retaliation also ensure additional terrorism. One guarantees the other. Violence, whether initial or retaliatory, augments the dilemma, and if the plain evidence has any significance at all, it would appear that violent reprisal is the standard and accepted reaction to terrorism.

In late June of 1971 about 10,000 Mexican students marched in protest over the government's continued incarceration of about fifty students imprisoned as a result of a violent leftist demonstration in 1968 in Mexico City, which resulted in fifty deaths. The protesters were marching directly into a well-laid trap. Their goal was Mexico City's flamboyant Monument of the Revolution, but they had covered only a small part of the way when riot police appeared, blocking the route of march.

When the great storm of protesters moved, the police fired volleys of tear gas, standard procedure against unarmed but large bodies of people. The tear-gas firing, however, was evidently a signal for what happened next.

On a side street where they had been parked, waiting, a line of buses abruptly disgorged scores of young men, mostly armed with the kind of bamboo poles used by the Japanese in their unique stave-fighting, but there was also a second wave, a reserve force, armed, more ominously, with pistols and carbines.

The police did nothing as the first wave of bamboo-swinging young men struck the foremost ranks of protesting students. The attackers repeatedly cried out, "*Halcones! Halcones!*" (Falcons! Falcons!) They were members of a Mexican rightist organisation numbering well into the thousands, called Falcons, who had attacked leftists before, particularly demonstrating students.

When about 300 demonstrators had been bloodily bludgeoned to the ground, and while other hundreds were fighting to get free of the mob and the confusion, the second wave of Falcons, with guns, appeared with military exactness, fired into the crowd, killing 9 students and wounding many more.

Denunciation was fierce; even government officials were of the opinion that the Falcons had been excessively brutal. But this may in many cases have been nothing more than political hypocrisy because someone with adequate military expertise had trained the Falcons, not only in stave-fighting, but also in close-order military tactics. Their attack was not as spontaneous as it was alleged to have been, otherwise, obviously, they would not have been waiting, armed and ready, in the buses which had transported them to the place where they could best attack the protesters. Nor would the police have stepped aside when the Falcons charged, refusing to intervene even when the victims of gunfire fell.

There was an aftermath which suggests that the Falcons were indeed operating with at least nominal official sanction. When the attack was over and many of the injured had gone to a nearby hospital for care, squads of Falcons walked into the emergency care units, rounded up all ambulatory protestors, and left with them. It was said at once that these prisoners would be murdered. They were not, but many eventually reached their homes barely able to stand. Again, the police did not intervene.

There was yet another aftermath. Student protesters, generally leftists, stated openly that if there should be another meeting between organised students and organised Falcons, the next time the students would also be armed, and thus the provocation, which was the original student demonstration, ensured retaliation by rightist Falcons, which in turn almost certainly guaranteed additional violence, as though the only recourse to violence was additional, probably greater, violence.

Terrorism is certainly not inherent in every organised act of violence; in fact genuine terrorists, the career nihilists in a country such as Mexico, are probably a very small proportion of the population. Nor is it what these people actually accomplish as individuals that can pose a peril to society or the nation, but what they can do as organised groups is another matter; and they have done it across the face of the modern world.

It may not be more than a matter of time, two years, five years, one decade, before, somewhere, in Latin America, the Middle East or elsewhere, they actually do achieve control of a country as they sought to do, and failed dismally at, in Jordan, or as they sought to do in Uruguay, and came uncomfortably close to doing.

If this opportunity appears it can certainly be expected that terrorists throughout the world will gravitate towards it, exactly as they did in Uruguay. When there are enough of them, which there may very well be right now, and when the prospects of an accomplishment are certain, some country will fall to nihilists. If this appears too far afield for credence, it might be well to recall that up until 1970 it was a confident aphorism among anti-leftists that no nation had ever, through free-choice elections, seated a Communist in a Presidential Palace. That year Chile did. Salvador Allende did not survive; many national leaders do not, and in places such as Chile or Uruguay pure politics have less to do with their decline than do social and economic dilemmas which have been accumulating for generations. But for the terrorists the issue is not politics, it is simply destruction, and no society, Uruguayan, Chilean, or Israeli, can cope with the snowballing disenchantment unless it takes action. If, for example, Israel had resolved the Ikrit-Berem dilemma with the same expedition it showed the world in the Six-Day-War, there would no longer be an Ikrit-Berem problem. Unfortunately, governments move with the speed of molasses in January, which is precisely what will ensure that terrorists will eventually stage-manage a successful take-over; that, and the clear fact that, to-date, society's answer to violence is greater violence, a suspension of civil rights, an exaltation of the praetorians, and an attempt to crush dissidence by the identical lack of reason which ensured dissidence in the first place.

TEN

Black Pantherism

Originally, Black Pantherism was an exclusive United States phenomenon. Its function was to unify black opposition to the United States white majority, to demonstrate negro opposition to white oppression, to encourage violent defiance, and to agitate for 'black power', which was a myth everywhere except in black communities because negroes have historically lacked the numerical weight and the economic strength to exert real power, without the sympathy and support of whites.

Black Pantherism advocated militancy with a viable series of objectives, quite a number of which, beyond provoking violence, had no real objectives at all, as though violence were an end in itself.

As an organisation which originally consisted largely of terrorists, the Black Panther group did succeed in polarising a great amount of black dissatisfaction, particularly among ghetto urban blacks, and most especially among blacks whose frustrations and intellectual heritage have prevented them from achieving what others, both whites and blacks, have achieved. But the concept of pantherism was not new. It was basically a search for identity; a compulsion to act out aggravations which have beset all ghetto deprivees since the Christian minority met secretly in the Roman catacombs to organise against 'the system'.

In the United States pantherism synthesised black opposition and defiance. It encouraged black sociopaths to become terrorists. It helped create an environment of un-reason. In the city of Los Angeles as many as 150 murders were committed in one day, a great proportion of them being committed by blacks, and police investigations have encountered as a motive for this butchery, the unreasoning racial bias most militantly advocated by pantherism.

United States pantherism provided a catalyst for the previously splintered, incohesive but nonetheless very real and generations-old basic racial antagonisms, not exclusively in Los Angeles, not even exclusively in the United States South where black oppression originated and most stubbornly endured. In late 1972 the police of Chicago, which lies equally as distant from Los Angeles and the United States South, arrested five blacks and took into 'protective custody' a sixth black for questioning in connection with a series of pointless murders of whites, and during the course of the ensuing investigation it was discovered that a super-secret organisation known as 'De Mau Mau' existed, whose express purpose was the indiscriminate murder of white people. According to an informant, recruits for this organisation were accepted only providing they had killed a white person, or who were willing to commit such a slaying in the company of a 'De Mau Mau' companion.

A result of police probing brought to light the explanation for an entire series of theretofore unexplained murders. In May, 1972, a 19-year-old University sophomore was shot to death for no apparent reason as he stood along a highway near Carbondale, Illinois. Three months later a United States soldier standing beside an arterial throughway on the outskirts of Chicago, was shot to death by a gunman in a speeding car, and that same week a man named Stephen Hawtree was shot to death, along with his wife and teenage son, for no discernible reason. There were other equally brutal and senseless murders within easy driving distance of Chicago which defied explanation until the existence of the 'De Mau Mau' organisation was revealed.

According to a black informant the 'De Mau Mau' organisation was initially formed among black United States servicemen whose objective at that time was 'fragging', or using fragmentation grenades, to kill white officers of the armed forces. These discharged black servicement carried their private war into civilian life with them, encouraged in this by the black militancy of pantherism. The result was indiscriminate murder.

It was alleged that there were 400 members of the Chicago unit of the 'De Mau Mau' organisation. If this were true then plausibly the

Chicago police as well as the authorities of Cook County, in which Chicago is located, could provide motives for a total of 400 murders.

It was said that this ultra violent pantherist group had a nationwide membership of almost 5,000 blacks — which it possibly did not have — yet there were almost certainly no fewer than 5,000 black killers, actual or potential, in the United States, affiliated or not affiliated with groups such as the 'De Mau Mau', whose motivation as killer-terrorists achieved its impetus and inspiration from the nihilist Black Panther platform and policies.

White back-lash from this kind of violent black racism ultimately resulted in the slaying of a number of Panther leaders and the imprisonment of others. Eventually pantherism in the United States became less overtly violent, although it never abandoned its fundamental terrorist tenets, and the slayings which subsequently occurred were undertaken with more expertise and sophistication.

The single act which did most to turn even many responsible United States blacks against Panther terrorism occurred on 7th August, 1971, in the Northern California (Marin County) courtroom of Judge Harold J. Haley, who was to preside at the trial of a black prison inmate named James D. McClain, who was charged with feloniously attacking a prison guard.

A fellow inmate of California's San Quentin prison, of McClain, George Jackson, who was originally incarcerated for robbery but who was subsequently involved in the stabbing of a guard at Soledad Prison in Southern California, was transferred from Soledad to San Quentin in July. In August George Jackson's brother, 17-year-old Jonathan Jackson, took up residence in San Francisco to be near George. When Jonathan arranged to visit George, he was accompanied by a *cafe-au-lait* woman, gaunt of build, tall and quiet, who waited outside.

What occurred at these meetings was subsequently to be a matter of considerable conjecture, but whatever the Jacksons discussed, on the morning of 7th August when Judge Haley's tribunal was opened to the public, at the trial of James D. McClain, with Harold Haley on the bench, McClain, his attorney and two witnesses to the alleged stabbing, Ruchell McGee and William Christmas, at their table, and with Assistant County Prosecutor Gary Thomas in place, youthful Jonathan Jackson entered the courtroom carrying a valise.

An armed officer saw Jonathan Jackson take a seat near the rear of the courtroom among other spectators, and started towards him. Young Jackson arose, drew an automatic carbine from the valise, waved it back and forth and cried out: "This is it!" Jackson then took three more weapons from the valise, one for McClain, the defendent, and a gun each for the two witnesses, Christmas and McGee.

One weapon, a shotgun, was taped to Judge Haley's body with the muzzle beneath Haley's chin. Assistant prosecutor Thomas, and three female jurors were made hostages, and along with Judge Haley, were marched out of the courtroom. No one interfered. In the corridor a number of stunned bystanders watched as the blacks took their hostages to a lift.

On the ground floor more bystanders saw the hostages marched from the lift and out of the building to a light delivery van where they were pushed inside.

Two Marin County police cars appeared, blocking the parking area exit. At once gunfire erupted inside the van. The blacks, convinced they were not going to escape despite their success to this point, detonated the shotgun taped to the judge's body. Harold Haley was killed instantly by the decapitating blast. Prosecutor Thomas wrenched a weapon from one of his captors and in that confined space managed to fire seven times before being himself cut down by bullets in the heart and spine.

In the wild shoot-out which ensued, James McClain, William Christmas and young Jonathan Jackson were killed by police, while Ruchell McGee was shot in the chest. McGee subsequently recovered, as did Prosecutor Gary Thomas, henceforth paralysed from the waist down. None of the other hostages were seriously injured.

George Jackson, the brother for whom young Jonathan Jackson had so much admiration, learned of Jonathan's slaying the same day it happened while in his San Quentin cell. After some days of intense despair George Jackson appeared in the prison exercise yard with a pistol — said to have been smuggled in to him by his white lawyer — and while seeking to escape, was shot to death.

George Jackson was sent for burial to Illinois in the first week of September, 1971, and at once the fury caused by Judge Haley's wanton slaying, which found differing degrees of expression all across the United States in the white communities, had its counterpart in the black communities. Terrorist retaliation for the slaying of the Jackson brothers, McClain and Christmas, was swift and virulent. Particular targets of black terrorists were policemen and police stations.

A group calling itself the 'George L. Jackson Assault Squad of the Black Liberation Army' enticed the police from their Ingleside police station in San Francisco the night following Jackson's funeral in Illinois, by detonating a bomb at a nearby branch bank. When the police rushed to investigate, a band of blacks entered the precinct station and amid the subsequent indiscriminate shooting, one man thrust a shotgun through a window, pulled the trigger, killing police sergeant John V. Young and wounding another officer nearby.

The terrorists fled and the following day sent letters to the newspapers saying the Ingleside attack was in retaliation for "the recent intolerable political assassination of Comrade George L. Jackson in particular and the inhumane torture in POW camps [i.e. prisons] in general."

The outburst of violence which followed in the wake of Judge Harold Haley's murder involving blacks had a predictable aftermath. The Haley affair had stunned and outraged most Americans, not all white, and not all pro-establishment; the ensuing fresh wave of violence brought to a climax the resentment, antagonism, and the candid outrage which had been steadily accumulating nationwide, with another predictable result — retaliation, often disguised as legal process or, in the event of black terrorists being slain, which happened not altogether infrequently, as justifiable self-defence, eliminated a number of pantherist doctrinaires. But while this employing force against force convinced leaders of the United States black constituency that they could not win in any such competition (and they subsequently toned down their overt policies) as a matter of fact every large black community in the United States continued to stockpile armaments, form secret societies of assassins, organise bomb and sniper squads, and generally subscribe to terrorism.

It was never determined, nor probably will it ever be determined, how many terrorists succumbed in the United States black communities to the increasingly virulent leftist and nihilist philosophies, and yet Black Pantherism did not remain an exclusive American phenomenon. Non-black dissenters displaying the particular coiffure of radical blacks, the 'Afro', or 'Natural', have appeared in such disparate places as Japan and Israel. This does not mean they were sympathetic to the ideals of United States black terrorists, and undoubtedly in many cases it did not even mean they were confirmed dissenters, but many of them were activists.

What pantherism accomplished was to create another axis, this time in the United States black communities, where radical polemecists could solicit support. Overseas-pantherism reflected less sympathy for United States blacks than it reflected indigenous dissent; Iraeli activists, even when they adopted the Black Panther symbol and name, and imitated the exaggerated hair-dos of United States pantherists, probably knew less and cared less about alleged oppression of blacks in North America than the average erudite, older Israeli, who at least read newspapers. But pantherism offered a number of adaptable symbols and for a while at least Black Panthers held a place of notoriety among dissenters and those whose psychoses required borrowed simulacra, perferably violent ones, identified readily with United States black terrorists.

But essentially, pantherism was a rallying factor. Until its advent United States black extremists actually did not have a genuine organisation of any size or substance. They had any number of neighbourhood, regional associations, weak in numbers, often at war with one another, and always woefully under-financed; hardly worth the effort of leftist and extremist infiltrators. With the advent of the nation-wide Black Panther movement, black revolutionaries were able to join and actively support a strong, cohesive, aggressive, and militant, establishment, which was worth the infiltration efforts of extremists.

As a terrorist order, pantherism provided a catalyst. Thousands of black activists became Black Panthers. Those previously lacking goals or direction, found these objectives within the organisation. Hundreds became associated with the assassination squads. Blacks as well as whites were slain in order of Panther leaders. Among the subsidiary units and regional Black Panther cells were dedicated fanatics amenable to any order. These people could be sent anywhere to commit murder or to encourage violence and destruction.

They were not very much different from those other, much earlier fanatics of Syria, the *hashashin*, nor, for that matter, a host of other extremists down the centuries, at least in their dedication and deadliness.

United States Panthers were originally dedicated to organising and unifying black opposition to the white establishment. They were zealous in their violent denunciation of what they insisted was the double standard of United States law and United States institutions, and were unyielding advocates of black supremacy, black separatism, and the destruction of white people, white rule, and white institutions.

Their concern with black supremacy and separatism went no further than the national boundaries of the United States, at first, but later, with the success of the movement making possible a more far-reaching philosophy, leaders of the movement had visions of a hemispheric black union reaching as far as the Caribbean, for its numbers, strength, and its support.

But originally and basically black pantherism in the United States was indigenous; it actually remained so, despite the loftier aspirations of a few good organisers and a few visionaries. When it was initiated elsewhere, as in Israel, there was no actual affinity; United States blacks probably understood less about Middle-eastern problems than anyone outside of, possibly, Africa itself. They took no steps to form an alliance with Israeli panthers, did nothing actually, to strengthen their international image, the way other terrorist organisations had done under similar circumstances, and chose to remain discriminatory in their racial insularity, ignoring their Middle-Eastern imitators.

They were an exclusive United States phenomenon and chose to remain so. Their terrorism, noticeably leftist-oriented, became formidable only after the panther movement was infiltrated by trained terrorists, otherwise, it was just as deadly, but in a manner which featured almost no cohesiveness; which in fact was almost totally lacking, in the beginning, even among black members of regional affiliates, with the result being that individual panthers embarked upon bloody but often unauthorised personal vendettas.

But black pantherism, like airplane highjacking, had its period of international notoriety, and those who, in such places as Israel, saw in pantherism an expression of defiance, of resistance by the oppressed, during the apex of this notoriety, emulated it.

A young Sephardic Jew, Saadya Marciano, born in France but a resident of Israel — more accurately, a resident of Jerusalem's teeming Musrara slum-ghetto — organised the Israeli Black Panther association, adopting the clenched-fist salute, among other pantherisms, and ultimately professed that pantherism in Israel had signed up no less than 9,000 members in its first year (1971).

Premier Golda Meir warned of internal violence which could be "rooted in social problems and would be more frightening than any war on [Israel's] borders."

The reference to "social problems" was valid; Israel, geared to war for 23 years, since ahieving independence, had experienced a burgeoning trade deficit, existed under the heaviest burden of taxation in the world, had an enormous poverty and welfare problem, but most ominous of all, the Sephardim, or Jews of Asiatic or African origin, while comprising almost 70 percent of the national population, as opposed to the European Jews, the Ashkenazim, who ruled Israel, controlled the wealth, industry, politics, army, and the government, existed at, or below, the poverty level, and saw themselves as an oppressed people. Not an oppressed minority, as the blacks of the United States saw themselves, but as a discriminated-against, deprived majority.

It was this sense of oppression that encouraged Israel's Black Panthers to identify with pantherism in the United States.

Saadya Marciano's Israeli panthers demonstrated against such things as sub-standard housing and police brutality, the same things United States panthers had demonstrated against, but, initially at any rate, Israel's malcontents were not noted for serious terrorism, although they clashed with police, and caused consternation in many quarters, where the prospect of Jews fighting among themselves caused dread and anxiety.

There was reason to expect trained terrorists to infiltrate the ranks as well as the upper-echelon councils of Israel's Black Panthers. Not United States Black Panthers, at least not in appreciable numbers although it is entirely plausible that leftist blacks from the United States might appear, but certainly, with the Middle East, generally, in ferment, and with Israel in particular, a target for leftist agitators, trained terrorists could scarcely be expected to overlook this opportunity to establish a foothold in one Middle Eastern nation long viewed by all leftists, and many terrorists, as their particular foe.

Pantherism, while no longer as outwardly virulent even in the United States as it was a decade ago, nevertheless remains a force among terrorist organisations. Its underground has not diminished, and its racism has continued undiluted. In recent years in the United States there has been a concerted attempt to change the fanatical and bloody image, projecting a benignity which has been reflected in community projects and the talking-down of violence, with no actual corresponding softening of the hard line among those at all leadership levels — the objective being to lull "whitey". To a degree this projection has succeeded. The number of murders of whites by blacks attributed to overt pantherism, has lessened. Not the numbers of such murders, but the reasons attributed to them.

United States pantherism began to assume a degree of sophistication when the United States white community began to react to violence with greater violence. The terrorist squads went underground. No great amount of perspicacity was required for the Panther leadership to appreciate that 25 million United States blacks could not expect to triumph over 180 million whites, not academically, not politically, and certainly not numerically nor violently.

But pantherism, in the United States as a virulent terrorism, and elsewhere in the world as a rallying factor, or symbol, for terrorists, did not die, it simply adapted to the changing times, as did the Arab-world's terrorist organisations, or as did the *Rengo Sekigun*, the Red Army of Japan, whose leadership disappeared behind the closed borders of Asia's increasing coterie of leftist nations.

ELEVEN

Ireland's Classic Terrorism

In Latin America, the Middle East, in Asia and Africa, terrorism has been sensitive to politics and economics. In a great many places terrorism has waxed and waned according to political and economic fluctuations, things which have historically influenced the lives of all people. But in Northern Ireland (Ulster) terrorism has for a number of years been grounded in a different duality, a kind that is a lot less susceptible to manipulation — emotionalism and idealism.

Pragmatic terrorism has been overcome by practical methods. Uruguay's urban terrorists, the Tupamaros, could be crushed despite Cuban, Chilean, and other outside aid, by a combination of raw force and economic embargoes. At least the Tupamaro organisation could be shattered and demoralised by embargoes, plus bullets, but in Northern Ireland economics have not visibly influenced the terror while that other factor, raw force, has done everything but encourage a lessening of the horror.

When unreasoning emotion has been the basis for terror the ordinary and accepted methods of control and suppression have not succeeded. Armed opposition has never been very successful as an answer to emotional activism.

Besides the damage to property, valued at about £40 million, sustained between mid-1969 and early 1972, Northern Ireland, which was never a very affluent region, sank into a deeper and more unresponsive emotional fanaticism each time armed force sought to compel order. As for economic sanctions, the authorities have not really had to employ them because the Irish themselves have quite thoroughly devastated their own territory, with terrible results, in a classic example of emotional terrorism, the kind which is blind to the normal moralities; i.e. children, the bewildered elderly, women, even animals, have been indiscriminately shot to death.

Belfast, a city of nearly half a million people, became a shambles. The years of terrorism have left scars that decades of peaceful co-existence between Catholics and Protestants will not ameliorate. In those four years more than 1,000 bombs have contributed to the gutting of Ulster's capital. There has been no section of the city which has not suffered. Buildings where people normally congregate, cinemas and pubs, markets, meeting halls, even department stores and hotels, have been blasted. Ulster's buses have been repeatedly attacked with the result that none operate in some areas, while in other areas they do not function after sundown, which seriously cripples the business areas, which must depend to a considerable extent for their survival upon commuting customers.

The number of killings increases weekly with most of them occurring in Belfast. In the Catholic communities where British troops have had to be most active in their thankless efforts to compel peace, and where the Irish Republican Army (I.R.A.) has most violently opposed this effort, guerrilla warfare of the most savage kind has continued over the years with a deadly result, not only in lives, but in devastation. Entire streets of working-class residences have been abandoned, gutted by bombings, and made untenable by constant sniping and organised terrorism.

In the centre of Belfast, the economic heart of Ulster, as well as of Belfast, I.R.A. bombs have ruined the city's largest department store, the railroad depot, and entire blocks of commercial establishments. Trade has been curtailed, unemployment, always one of Northern Ireland's most serious and chronic troubles, has soared. Belfast's shipyards, at one time an important source of foreign exchange, as well as the largest single source of employment, have drastically reduced their operation; ship owners do not send their vessels to an area where terrorists with a penchant for detonating gelignite employ their variety of terrorism indiscriminately and unpredictably.

No segment of Ulster's economy has not been seriously injured, even the once rather frenetic and uninhibited night-life has all but died, the result of a steadily worsening economic situation, of course, but equally as much the result of the I.R.A.'s established practice of pitching bombs into crowded places.

Ulster's tourist trade, another former source of much-needed foreign capital, has been dead on its feet for several years. The largest hotel in Northern Ireland, Belfast's Grand Central, went out of business in the autumn of 1971, and was subsequently reactivated as the headquarters for a different kind of guests, a battalion of the British army. The palatial, very modern Europa hotel opened for business in August of 1973, with one paying guest. It has been bombed eight times.

Belfast's public services continued to function, which amounted to a minor miracle; the fire brigades were heroic, frequently battling infernos which made firemen ideal targets for snipers by outlining them on otherwise dark nights in dazzling flames. Police protection atrophied in urban Ulster as British troops assumed the role of peace-keepers. Ulster's one-time tough and no-nonsense Royal Constabulary corps, largely Protestant, and with an excellent record as a peace-keeping unit was relegated to a largely secondary or spectator status by the British army. But there has always been a great difference between police and army methods and techniques of keeping the peace. Army methods have been essentially forceful, leading to legal prosecution and punishment. In one month, July of 1973, terrorists from both sides killed 39 people, Protestants and Catholics, under the nose of the army. There have been instances of Protestant and Catholic terrorists wantonly hurling bombs and sniping into mixed crowds in downtown Belfast, killing their own kind.

A clear understanding of what the Irish refer to as 'their troubles' has allegedly existed in Ulster (Northern Ireland) as well as in the Republic of Ireland (Southern Ireland) for a generation and a half, and yet rarely has *any* Irish commentator been able to clearly or lucidly project an explanation which makes much sense to the rest of the world, where Ireland's 'troubles' do not appear as terrorism, so much as they appear to be civil war — which they are, and are not. Particularly, has understanding of 'the troubles' been muddled and obscure in the United States, where a considerable flow of financial support, especially for the Irish Republican Army, has been forthcoming. At one time partisan United States aid in the more tangible form of weapons, was a factor, but when the United States government outlawed this kind of support, aid became almost exclusively financial, which of course amounts to the same thing since the world's arms-dealers have always accepted United States dollars.

In England, which belatedly felt the exported fury of Irish bombers, the understanding was clearer, but it was also harsh in its condemnation of the terrorist tactics of Ireland's fanatics, and impatient with Ireland's uninspired efforts at seeking a solution.

Elsewhere in the world, the consensus was unflattering. The Irish appeared as a collective, ethnic example of emotional immaturity, of ethnic instability.

Fundamentally, 'the troubles' arose over the 1921 partition of Ireland. The island was divided into the Irish Free State, to the south, consisting of 26 counties, preponderantly Catholic and certainly dominated by Catholics, and Northern Ireland (namely the province of Ulster) to the north, mostly Protestant, consisting of 6 counties, which chose to remain a part of the United Kingdom.

Subsequently many Irish, largely Catholics, and the outlawed Irish Republican Army, which was well rooted in the south, undertook by terrorism to force the United Kingdom to relinquish Ulster so that it could then be incorporated by force into the Irish State.

Northern Ireland's half-million Catholics, encouraged by nationalists from Southern Ireland, denounced alleged Protestant discrimination against them. Ulster's Protestants were a clear majority of no less than one million. Denunciation led to public demonstrations, which led to public brawls, and by 1969 the situation was serious enough for the British Government to dispatch troops to prevent what predictably could have resulted in a shocking massacre of the activist Catholics, and their sub-rosa allies of the I.R.A.

The British Government urged Ulster's leadership to inaugurate specific reforms which granted the Catholic minority equal rights. All Catholic demands were met. The trouble could have ended then and there — except for one element: the illegal Irish Republican

Army, which had been the lodestar of Irish activists for many years, and whose particular foe had always been the British Home Government, and its enforcement complement, the British Army.

The I.R.A. was dedicated to a free and unified Ireland, regardless of whether or not the majority of Ulstermen elected to remain a part of Great Britain. Also, taking the major credit for Ulster's capitulation to Catholic demands, and encouraged by this capitulation to believe they could finally force unification of the north with the south, the I.R.A.'s leadership increased all subversive activity in the North, propagandised the Catholic minority, and steadily expanded its influence. By baiting British troops, the I.R.A. managed to acquire some excellent martyrs. The entire affair was very professionally orchestrated; in the end those Catholics the troops had initially been sent to protect, undertook to assassinate those same protectors with weapons supplied by the Irish Republican Army, and the predominately Protestant Royal Ulster Constabulary corps, was not encouraged to participate in the ensuing guerilla action between the British army and the I.R.A.

An erosion of law and order inevitably ensued, exactly in accordance with I.R.A. wishes. Murder of Protestants, for no other reason than because of their protestantism, was encouraged in the Catholic enclaves by I.R.A. subversives. The assassination of British soldiers was also encouraged and these men, whose duty in Ulster was thoroughly unrewarding and completely frustrating, ultimately became the targets even of small, rock-throwing children. Their restraint, their superlative discipline, the products of an unexcelled historic tradition, was unequalled in the history of terrorist confrontations. Making their position even less enviable was the fact that while their comrades were being slain daily by snipers and bombers, the British Home Government did not in principal object to the unification of Northern and Southern Ireland. Britain's two political parties, one Conservative, one Labour, agreed to unification providing Ulster chose to become a part of the Republic of Ireland, but not if the North was coerced by the I.R.A. into acquiescence and unification.

This enlightened viewpoint was not entirely altruistic. Ulster, even before the terrible and widespread devastation and demoralisation, was considered a poverty-area. The British Government had been subsidising Northern Ireland to the extent of approaching £140 million annually for some time, therefore, not only the soldiers in Ulster, but the tax-paying general public of Britain's other areas, within the United Kingdom, became bitterly disenchanted. In a poll, 59 percent of the British public favoured immediate withdrawal of all troops, and that, of course, had always been the desire of the I.R.A. which could then turn its terrorism against the Protestants and, hopefully, compel unification of Ulster with the Republic of the South.

Meanwhile, the terrorism increased. In order to avoid being shot down, British patrols had to shoot out street lights at night. During daylight hours they were able to compel order only in groups, and because they had been forbidden to fire where they were crowds, British soldiers were killed by terrorists who hid in crowds.

As conditions worsened, the desperate leaders of Northern Ireland had to do as was done in Canada, and elsewhere, when terrorism could not be contained by orthodox methods; Ulster's government inaugurated police-state methods. Hundreds of Catholics were rounded up and incarcerated without due process and without trials, an act which enraged even many Protestants in both Ulster and Eire. This Special Powers Act was reminiscent of democracy's breakdown elsewhere in the face of widespread, virulent terrorism. There had to be a better way, but the check-and-balance system did not demonstrate it, and meanwhile, Ulster reeled under mounting lawlessness, destitution and demoralisation which, after almost half a decade of terrorism, made it impossible to convict terrorists because no witness would appear against them.

One example of the I.R.A.'s systematic suppression of those courageous enough to appear as witnesses occurred in Belfast when a bus-driver who was summoned to testify against terrorists who had attacked his vehicle, left his house on the appointed day, and was shot dead in the doorway by a waiting assassin. Not many other bus-drivers, or others who were not bus-drivers, failed to understand the clear meaning of this act.

Terrorists of both factions successfully carried their savagery into homes, schools, churches, stores and even hospitals. Further, not all the murders were political. Gunmen bent on robbery proliferated. Killers with personal grudges killed scores of people. Ulster became an area susceptible to roving gangs, and communities such as Belfast and Londonderry became urban jungles.

In mid-1972 the Provisional Wing, a particularly savage, leftist segment of the I.R.A. killed 9 people and injured 130 more in the centre of Belfast by exploding 22 bombs in one day. Public reaction was swift and condemnatory, and British authorities moved at once against known and suspected Provisional members, called 'Provos', of the I.R.A. with the expressed intention of destroying the terrorist "capacities of the Provisional I.R.A.".

For once even I.R.A. sympathisers in both Ulster and Eire were willing for British army intervention to succeed. Ireland's Roman Catholic primate, Cardinal Conway, as well as Eire's Prime Minister, tough, quick-tempered John Lynch, and the efficient and likeable William Whitelaw, British administer in Ulster, called for an end to the terrorism, and this sort of thing could have caused a scaling down of the violence. It would not have resolved the issues at all, but would have caused a lessening of the violence simply because the great majority of Irish people, regardless of religious or political affiliation, seemed to be sufficiently outraged to demand an end of the terrorism.

But the Irish Republican Army, a successful terrorist organisation since 1919, could not be vanquished easily, in a part of the world where poverty has certainly inspired a great amount of opposition to all law and order.

The I.R.A., although only recently catapulted into prominence after more than a decade of relative obscurity was always a unique terrorist organisation in many ways. For one thing, although it established contacts with other world-wide terrorist organisations, and had a strong leftist taint, the Irish Republican Army remained exclusively Irish in all departments. Foreign influence has been minimal, and yet such diverse 'sympathisers' as Libya's firebrand President, Muammar Kaddafi, and Dutch, Belgian and German arms dealers, as well as several Red-bloc sources, have supplied arms, and in some cases, funds, to enable the outlawed I.R.A. battalions to function. Kaddafi's reason, stated in 1972, was blunt.

He wanted to arm "Irish revolutionaries to fight British imperialists". Other sympathisers were equally as ignorant of the actual situation, but in the case of most arms suppliers the reason was more basic: they sold arms to the I.R.A. for money.

With adequate sources for armament, the I.R.A. rapidly increased in size and power, but it appeared not to function as a complete military organisation, and this hampered efforts to destroy it. There was a military-style chain of command.

Top-echelon leadership consisted of a supreme council, rather like a senior military command-staff, which was responsible for inaugurating and overseeing all terrorist activity in both the north and the south of Ireland. This council had its headquarters in Eire, in comparatively safe Dublin. At the field-level, where orders from the council were implemented, the actual methods to be employed in the implementation were left to the discretion of field commanders, but with the council retaining full veto powers over regionally-sponsored violence.

I.R.A. battalions, such as the tough, fanatical Ardoyne unit, consisted of about 250 members. Brigade commanders acted in a liaison capacity between the council and battalion commanders, who in turn relayed instructions to company commanders.

There was no officer corps as such. There were no non-commissioned officers. Titles were not based, as in an army, on rank, but rather on specialities. A man who threw grenades was not a corporal, sergeant, or lieutenant, he was a grenade-man. Task forces were not isolated or separate units. Specialists were detached from general companies to be temporarily assigned to sniping, assassination, or bomb-planting special groups, and upon completion of an assignment returned to their general companies.

The I.R.A. had strict, even brutal, rules of secrecy and deportment. Drinking while on duty could be punishable by execution. Among the Provisional faction savage beatings for minor infractions were commonplace, but generally, I.R.A. members had a fanatic's loyalty.

In Northern Ireland a lifelong activist named Seumus Twomey assumed leadership of the leftist Provisionals when the former leader, Joe Cahill was taken into custody during a successful attack upon a gun-running freighter from Libya in Muggort's Bay off

Ireland's southern coast. Twomey unleashed a wave of terror beginning in July of 1972 to prove his ability, ending a very brief British-sponsored truce, and true to I.R.A. policy, the organisaiton's penchant for secrecy, absolutely essential for the survival of most terrorist establishments, enabled the terrorists to complete satisfactorily all of their major strikes, then to fade into the civilian environment practically without loss.

Gerry Adams, a former bartender, shared overall leadership with Twomey. Adams was 23 years of age at the time he became a leader, to Seumus Twomey's nearly twice as many years. Adams was a product of the I.R.A.'s youth movement, the Fianna. He was also somewhat of a thorn in the flesh to the Dublin-based council because of his savage, often unauthorised strikes, in Ulster.

Twomey and Adams have sanctioned the shooting off of the kneecaps of members accused of infractions. Both are feared by those within the ranks of the I.R.A. and others who are not affiliated, and with good reason. Neither leader, Twomey or Adams, has ever hesitated to authorise murder. Any I.R.A. member who visits with, accepts a drink from, or even in some cases has been seen conversing with British soldiers, is summarily executed.

The I.R.A. maintains semi-military courts. The sentences handed down by these tribunals are often fatally relevant. Those condemned for talking too openly about the I.R.A., or who have been sentenced for talking with British soldiers, are shot through the mouth.

The I.R.A.'s greatest asset has been its insularity. Secrecy is paramount. Members in mufti are everywhere, and while it is a foregone fact that Britain's MI6 has penetrated at all levels, nevertheless the kind of para-military organisation that operates as does the I.R.A., very often with neighbours being members without either one suspecting this of the other, has always been the most difficult kind of an establishment to destroy. It also increases the difficulty when most members are fanatics who, singly and in small groups, have often embarked upon suicide assignments where foreknowledge has not been enough to prevent a mass-slaying, although it frequently has resulted in the death of the fanatics.

The other side of the coin was the U.D.A., the Protestant counterpart in Northern Ireland of the I.R.A. The U.D.A. — Ulster Defence Association — headed by a 13-man Defence Council, has, again like the I.R.A., two principal leaders in Ulster, one was Tommy Herran, a youthful garage manager, while the other was an older man, John Anderson, who also presided over the council.

The U.D.A., in fact, while patterning itself along military lines, complete with military ranks and titles, which was different from the I.R.A. in this respect, actually used the I.R.A. as the model for most of its organisational structuring. It also borrowed much of the I.R.A.'s brutal methods of punishment for the violators of its rules, and employed many I.R.A. tactics when it struck Catholic communities.

One thing the U.D.A. did not have to borrow from the I.R.A. was the equally fanatical dedication of its Protestant members.

The U.D.A. claimed a membership in Northern Ireland of 50,000 which was conceivably not too high. These people, although pro-British to the extent of clinging stubbornly to their affiliation with the United Kingdom, were almost as much a source of trouble to the British troops, as the troops were to the U.D.A. Both groups, the I.R.A. and the U.D.A., were terrorist in mentality. Of the hundreds of dead Protestants and Catholics throughout Ulster, many have been so terribly cut up, shot up, and bombblackened, that identification has been almost impossible.

Terrorists operating exclusively on totally unrestrained emotion have been notorious for butchering victims in this fashion.

Force alone cannot stifle the variety of partisan terrorism which has devastated Ulster. Conciliation alone cannot put an end to it either. Uninhibited emotionalism, like pure idealism, has never responded satisfactorily to general mediation for any notable length of time. In the case of Northern Ireland the solution may only lie in an overwhelming sense of revulsion by both Catholic and Protestants, or it may lie in exhaustion, but obviously the factors which have compelled atrophy in other areas — economics and politics — have not worked here, where terrorists have succeeded in almost totally disrupting and destroying a province.

TWELVE

In the Van and Wake Of Terror

It has been said that behind the unreasoning fanaticism of every terrorist there is a totally rational person planning and directing.

Obviously, that has been true more often than not, and it need not apply exclusively to terrorists; a great number of people who have never been 'committed' have been manipulated.

For a decade and more the popular exhortation has been for more involvement, more commitment, more participation — to become a participant in the present, welcome commitment to a struggling ideology, realise individual fulfilment by becoming involved with the charismatic issues of the times.

Quite possibly if all human beings were capable of unbiased judgment and could be relied upon for balanced assessments — even their initial ignorance of a subject would not very seriously aggravate it — they would be more difficult to manipulate. They would not be as likely to accept patent propaganda, and they would possibly do nothing at all, before they would become involved as a result of the irrationality of emotional commitment.

Throughout the 'sixties and 'seventies those three words, commitment, involvement and participation, occasioned more aggravation, bitterness and confusion, not less. In the case of Northern Ireland they also occasioned more death and ruin.

A fair example of involved people whose emotions impaired their reason to the extent that they were manipulated, were thousands of Americans, mostly of Irish descent, who have for a number of years been funneling voluntary contributions through such 'front' organisations as New York's 'Irish Northern Aid Society', with the result that terrorism in Ulster has been able to survive and flourish.

More than half a million dollars in cash has been contributed annually. The more actively 'involved' Americans have financed gun-running. Their 'commitment' has been largely responsible for the successes of the Irish Republican Army, which is specifically an invading armed force whose intention has always been to coerce, to terrorise and to destroy. These were the same Americans who supported United States efforts in such places as Vietnam, Cambodia — and earlier, in the Second World War — of free people elsewhere to resist coercion through armed invasion.

The 'Irish Northern Aid Society', like dozens of other 'front' organisations was not organised, as its name might imply, to aid the people of Northern Ireland; its function was to elicit funds for the support of I.R.A. terrorists in Northern Ireland, whose clear objective was to kill, to destroy, to bring exhaustion through relentless terror, to all of Ulster.

Sympathy is an emotional response; at times it is a very commendable response. At other times, as in the case of Northern Ireland, sympathy or all emotional involvement that has resulted in American dollars ensuring the murder of people in their own land whose own 'involvement' has basically been that they have resisted armed outsiders, is absolutely contrary to the belief of most Americans.

American and other emotional involvement in Northern Ireland, has been cooly manipulated. Gun-running to Ireland from the United States, financed by involved Americans, has been fairly well eliminated through federal and state legal opposition, but it has not been eliminated elsewhere, and in other ways.

The German-owned 300-ton freighter, *Claudia*, operating under Green registry, was an example, in one recent trip, how volunteer-United States dollars have sought to perpetuate terrorism.

The *Claudia*, presumably engaged to pick up cargo at Cadiz on the southern coast of Spain, actually took on her load in the Mediterranean, south of Sicily, at a Libyan port. She then steamed back through the Strait of Gibraltar, and somewhat later, on a very dark night, the *Claudia* appeared off the headlands of southern Ireland, a rusty ghost in a choppy sea, whose entire odyssey had been monitored by Britain's intelligence establishment, all the way from Africa through the Straits (by submarine) to her destination at Muggort's Bay.

The Irish navy — a fishery patrol vessel and three minesweepers — quietly alerted well in advance, was positioned and waiting. When a large launch put to sea from Dungarvan Harbour on Eire's side of St George's Channel to rendezvous with the *Claudia*, the navy closed in. One warning shot was fired. The *Claudia* offered no resistance. An armed boarding party took into custody Joe Cahill, former commander of the I.R.A.'s Belfast Brigade, a Provo unit, along with five other upper-echelon I.R.A. leaders, and revealed the reason six important terrorist commanders had been on hand to welcome the *Claudia*: dozens of crates of grenades and mines, almost a ton of bomb-component explosives, 500 automatic weapons, pistols and rifles, and 25,000 rounds of ammunition, all paid for in cash by voluntary contributions, were in the *Claudia's* holds.

Obviously, not all outside aid has come from the United States. The second largest headache for every Prime Minister of Eire for over a hundred years, has been his foreign constituency. Naturalised and natural-born people of Irish descent all over the world, from Canada to Argentina, from Africa to Newfoundland, have demonstrated an affinity, largely emotional, for the 'Auld Sod', even though their nearest actual affinity was an emigrant-grandfather, even though they have never seen Ireland, and even though they have rarely been honestly or impartially informed concerning 'the troubles'.

But in the United States, at least, there has been a very large and powerful segment of affluent people of Irish descent for several generations whose tax-deductible donations have contributed enormously towards the deaths of bomb-shredded men, women and children in Northern Ireland. They have responded very well to the outcry for 'involvement' and 'commitment' by becoming vicarious terrorists. They have, in common with people of Irish descent the world over, responded with emotionalism to a cause that has little hope of being resolved as long as they continue to exhort, and support, terrorism.

They have evinced the basic necessity of all

terrorists — irresponsible emotionalism. They have been used, programmed and manipulated by leftist planners and directors, and they have also been coaxed into both supporting and advocating terrorism by rightist manipulators.

The Republic of Ireland's Prime Minister, John Lynch, offered an opinion which has been prevalent amongst knowledgeable outsiders as well as the responsible Irish for years. Speaking in the United States Lynch said, "People who contributed [to I.R.A. front organisations] are misinformed, misguided, and some are even subversive", but he did not advocate the cessation of financial aid; he suggested rather that those seeking to fund the rehabilitation of Ulster channel their aid through the International Red Cross rather than through sources which would spend it in Libya, Germany, Belgium or elsewhere, in the unclean business of clandestine gun-running, which was, of course, all well and good, except that those people who, through deliberate choice or emotional un-reason, have preferred to interpret 'involvement' in ways certain to prolong and aggravate 'the troubles', will continue to abet violence by supporting terrorism, and it has appeared over the years that these people are a majority. They most certainly have been in Northern Ireland, as well as in those world communities whose policies and preferences have been favourable to the promotion, and support, of terrorism.

It has been the deliberate terrorist functioning in the van of turmoil and disruption who has been best able to avoid orthodox restraint by using the laws of free societies as his best protection. Freedom of speech, for example, as well as the right of free assembly, have historically been his most valued tools. He has invariably denied these rights to others, both within his own organisation, and among the populaces he has, from time to time, achieved supremacy over, and this has, in its turn, resulted in some very spectacular and sanguine results in places where terrorism has not been able to acquire a solid mandate. Chile, in Latin America, has been a recent example. There, terrorism on the left evoked an overwhelming backlash of rightist terrorism, toppling the first freely-elected collectivist president since the advent of world leftism.

The element most responsible for that fiery confrontation between the terrorists of right and left in Chile was leftism's premature and patently impatient reach for complete power. There was never, from the beginning of leftist President Salvador Allende's assumption of power, a mandate. Leftism won a free election by a small margin. So small in fact that although it did achieve power, Chilean opposition was very great, and when the inevitable restrictions against the free functions of an independent people ensued, which have traditionally been the policy of restrictive governments of the left, or the right, even though they did not actually affect very many Chileans, the fact that they were inaugurated convinced Chileans, who have long been one of the most democratic people of South America, that worse was soon to come. In short order, then, the great minority became the activist great majority, with gory results. Terrorism was pitted against terrorism, and, as in Northern Ireland, those whose hands held the most and best weapons, accomplished the most thorough devastation, the basic difference being that in Chile outside influences, although ready, were unable to exert adequate counter-pressure in time, because, according to plan, the *coup* was swift, merciless, and overwhelming. It was a Chilean episode; the best leftism could offer against concerted military might, was small-arms opposition, individual assassination, and rhetoric, none of which was very effective against armour, aircraft, and the powerful rightist sentiment which had been steadily increasing for several years.

In the wake of the earlier leftist sophistry which, to some extent through intimidation, stage-managed Salvador Allende's confirmation in power, there was simply too much genuine and well-armed opposition. As in Jordan during the hey-day of the Palestinian terrorists, in the wake of too much subversion there was a stormy backlash which in Chile, as in Jordan, encouraged the unleashing of violent rightism. Terror faced terror, and, as has been the case in recent wars, those commanding the most devastating force, triumphed.

It succeeded in Jordan, in Uruguay, in Chile, but not in Ireland where the real preponderance of power was in the hands of the British army. There, both in the vanguard and in the wake of terror, under unique conditions which precluded the use of the kind of force necessary to compel peace and a return to order, the armour was certainly in evidence, but its presence alone could not compel a *detente*, something the terrorists were quite aware of.

In Chile, a savage backlash could triumph without causing many ripples in Europe. In Jordan, too, busy rightist terror, in the form of firing squads, could encourage a return to nationalism without causing much of an outcry elsewhere, but in Ireland, which is not just a British environ, but a part of the central and western European community of nations, removing the restraint from Britain's peace-compelling force would unleash a deluge of condemnation, and most certainly international terrorism, as well as a great majority of the leftist-oriented nations of Europe, plus a host of other countries, perhaps well-meaning but nevertheless sensitive to the current popular tendency throughout Europe, towards everyone minding everyone else's business as well as their own, would intervene in one way or another, and what was a deplorable situation, would then become something else — a potentially very dangerous situation.

The irony in Ulster has been that while the force to compel order has existed, ready and able to function, it simply dared not do so, which has left the terrorists almost a free field, and in the aftermath of devastation, it will most certainly fall to the British to finance the re-building of Northern Ireland. Those who could have compelled peace dared not do so, and in the wake of the ruin which they have been forced to witness, they will be required to spend even more money than the support of their armour in Ulster has cost, to re-create an area which has certainly been Britain's most unhappy and least compensatory adjunct. But Ulster certainly has been a splendid proving-ground for terrorists. Their expertise, for example, in the most advantageous uses of gelignite, reached a quite respectable sophistication. Their experiments in divisive rhetoric have certainly been productive; confusion, bewilderment, divided national and provincial leadership, north and south, have been endemic for years. The international relationship has been strengthened; the cooperation between North Africa, European, even Middle-Eastern, and Irish, terrorists has been confirmed, all of it most certainly adding to the coordinated effort of world-wide terrorism. Those who have envisaged this burgeoning international force for terror as perhaps more coincidental, or affinitively sympathetic, without also being susceptible to over-all direction, can find enough unsettling evidence to the contrary if they recall the words of International terrorism's Dr George Habash, or if they remembered the statements of any number of International Terrorism's surviving assassins, saboteurs, organisers, and acolytes. But most impressive of all, if they will consider that manipulation in the expert hands of terrorist leaders is a two-edged weapon which can, and has been used just as effectively to coordinate and organise terrorists, as it has been used to divide and bewilder and falsely inspire the opponents of terrorism.

Montevideo, March 1971:
Geoffrey Jackson, British
ambassador, sits in captivity
beneath an improvised five-
pointed star, the Tupamaro
symbol

Uraguyan police searching
for a Tupamaro tunnel

George Jackson, one of the 'Soledad' brothers

A Black Panther demonstration in New York, September 1971

THIRTEEN

Retaliation From The Right

One of the most improbable socio-political units in the modern world is the South American Republic of Chile, a nation whose length is 2,650 miles, whose average width is 110 miles, and where, in one day's driving, a person can motor to a ski resort through a heavy snowfall in the morning, and motor in the opposite direction in the afternoon, to any one of Chile's magnificent beaches, and swim under a blazing sun — and do both in July and August.

Chile has long been one of the most stable democratic nations of South America. Its fiscal policies have historically been sound, its politics viably nationalistic, its traditions and laws fair, equable, and largely conservative.

Over the past generation or so there has been the same decline of natural exports as in other lands. In Chile's case this has been largely nitrate, now produced synthetically, among other things. Also, as has occurred elsewhere, the frugal land has been required to support a steadily increasing population. Nonetheless, while the decline in exports was serious, innovative Chileans achieved increases in other export commodities such as copper, and also developed a wine industry, things which helped augment the nation's slender foreign exchange reserves.

Generally, Chile, as a fiscally sound and historically stable, trouble-free country, was accredited and respected throughout the world. Chilean currency, the *escudo*, enjoyed a degree of confidence in world money markets few other Latin American monetary mediums have consistently enjoyed.

Political stability was a matter of pride among Chileans, whose neighbours, Argentina, Bolivia, Peru, and more distantly, troubled

Uruguay, could certainly have envied up until very recent times. Chile's generals have made a particular point of maintaining the desirable division between the armed services and the civil government. Chile's military was the least politically involved in South America, for many decades.

In 1970, when Salvador Allende Cossens became President of Chile, the thrust of communism was strong throughout all Latin America. Uruguay's Tupamaros were flourishing, Cuba's Fidel Castro was busy exporting terror, and the left, which forced Salvador Allende's triumph in the Chilean elections, was ascendent. Chilean leftists supported Uruguay's Tupamaros; President Allende made Chile a haven for those engaged in subverting Uruguay. He supported Tupamaro terrorists in many ways, and as an avowed Marxist, it was his hope to see Uruguay become a communist stronghold in mainland South America. Allende, though, was a paradox. Although a professed leftist, he enjoyed wealth, gracious living, good liquor, and lovely women. He never affected the combat fatigue attire, the beard, the conspicuous display of weapons, or the beret, of other Latin-American leftists. When he was urged to establish a headquarters-residence in one of Santiago's *barrios*, where the poor lived, he declined. When he holidayed in Argentina, he missed no chance to revel at the casinos and dancehalls. He was an impeccable man, fastidious, immaculate, a lover of the good life, things which were not ordinarily part of a good revolutionary's philosophy. When he and his friend, Fidel Castro, were photographed in Havana at a leftist celebration, Salvador Allende alone among the hemisphere communist leaders, appeared in a white shirt, wearing a tie, with polished shoes and a tailored suit.

While he was actively engaged in supporting the overthrow of Uruguay's elected government with guns and money, and while he was encouraging the use of Chile as the sanctuary for terrorists from all parts of the world, was making Chile the staging area for Urugay's Tupamaro organisation, he was also appearing among non-communists as the typical 'establishment man', and it was not a ruse. Salvador Allende scorned leftism's rhetoric and crudity from the day of his inauguration to the day of his death three years later, preferring to fulfill his leftist destiny, not as a bearded, cigar-chewing *barbudo*, but as a gentleman, as a sophisticated Chilean of substance, as a patron of the arts, an individual of poise, and ironically it was this side of Salvador Allende's character that duped many Chileans into voting for him as the nation's Chief Executive. They would never have voted for the stereotyped leftist, the kind of man characterised by Fidel Castro and Che Guevara — unshorn, unshaven, dressed in rumpled green jungle fatigues, submachine gun slung over one shoulder, bombastic and menacing.

But an even deeper irony than Allende's duping of the Chilean electorate was Allende's duping of himself. There was no way under the sun for a urbane cosmopolitan to play in the same league with genuine leftists. Allende wrecked the Chilean economy, was fiscally irresponsible, and tried to create in democratic Chile a mainland Latin American communist hegemony. He did his utmost to destroy Chile's centuries-old traditions of freedom, individual enterprise, social order, and export-import balance, yet, excluding the explosive period shortly prior to his fall and death, Allende tried to achieve these things gradually, and with limited terrorism among his constituents, side-stepping the distasteful tactics of a Fidel Castro, and not once, up until the week of his death, was he able to genuinely accept the fact that leftism could not possibly triumph in any land with as strong a tradition of freedom as existed in Chile, unless it was forced on the nation by gun-barrel diplomacy.

There was no such thing as a gentleman leftist, any more than there was any such thing as an equalitarian terrorist. Salvador Allende, like Leon Trotsky, was an excellent theoretician, and a deplorable realist. His idea that totalitarian leftism could be enforced slowly, that a people with enduring traditions of individual rights and dignity could be gradually subjugated, and that leftism could function harmoniously in double harness with democracy, marked him for failure from the day he took office as Chile's president. Finally, when his gradual approach aroused the ire of all those home-grown and imported terrorists he had created a sanctuary for in Chile, Salvador Allende was manipulated by the real terrorists, was hurried along the road of the traditional, violent take-over, and when leftist repression threatened to swamp both Chile and Salvador Allende, the end had arrived.

In the ensuing backlash leftism was overcome by a popular uprising, one of the very few in Chile's history. Many of the terrorists fled. Allende, left practically alone in the Moneda Palace, said the only way the rightist coup's leaders, the army, could remove him from office would be in "*pijamas de madera*" — wooden pyjamas. The rightists took him at his word. When the rightists struck, in September 1973, with troops, tanks, aircraft and artillery, one of the first casualties was Salvador Allende Cossens, allegedly a suicide, carried from the national palace on a stretcher, his bullet-riddled body covered by a woollen poncho. He had said, back in 1970, that he would not be "just one more President of Chile", but that he would head "the first Chilean Government that will be authentically democratic, popular, national and truly revolutionary". Half facetiously he referred to his 'new epoch' as a "revolution of meat pies and red wine".

In the wake of his fall, and out of the pall of smoke still rising over Santiago, over all Chile in fact, a month and more after Allende's passing, the leftists viewed this additional failure of terrorism to take over a nation, as the result of one man's inability to face a fact Fidel Castro had sought to impress upon Allende: that the implementation of leftism can best be assured through a liberal use of gunbarrel-terrorism.

Allende, the gentleman of reason, wanted to prove that socialism and democracy were compatible, which of course had already been proved elsewhere, but the moment he allowed himself to be manipulated, not by socialists but by leftist terrorists, his own imports to Chile, he was diverted from socialism to communism, and was lost. Personal charisma, which Allende undoubtedly had, was not enough, when, at the polls, he aggregated only a fraction more than 36 percent of the popular vote. Added to this were Allende's impractical economics, needlessly induced shortages, and his stirring appeals to Chile's disenfranchised poor, who could never, by themselves, have sustained him in power.

Germany's revolutionary Rudi Dutschke put it aptly when he said Allende failed because he "tried to socialise the country . . . by the rules of bourgeois democracy". Allende might better have tried Castro's example of bombast and bullets. If he had then failed, as he probably would have, he could at least have done so in the traditional leftist manner, and as it was, Allende failed, not as a socialist, not as a practical communist, not even as a very believable leader of terrorists, although that is exactly what he was; he failed, as did Trotsky, because he was not ever really a practical revolutionary.

Salvador Allende very probably never really understood that in the game to which he had committed himself there has never been a place for gentlemen-idealists. He was the only one, and that was to be his death. His ringing promise to give Chile's poor a share of the national wealth was greeted with outcries of acclaim in the *barrios*. His assurance that the great landholdings would be broken up and redistributed, increased his popularity among Chile's have-nots. His cry for a re-distribution of national wealth, for government control of free enterprise, for the limitation of individual commercial endeavours, and handing over Chile's industry to the workers, brought him the noisy approbation of all Chile's irresponsibles.

As *El Companero Presidente* — Comrade President — he had the power to freeze prices and raise wages. The have-nots rejoiced, and when a cloud appeared upon the economic horizon in the form of shortages, occasioned because producers could not operate at a loss, Allende resolved it as many Latin-American leaders had done before him, by simply having more paper money printed.

Inflation struck. In the autumn of 1972, 250 Chilean escudos were required to purchase one United States dollar. Before the year ended it took 800 escudos to buy a dollar. The result was that Chileans, with more money than ever before, could purchase less; producers, unable to raise prices, lost money and went out of business, the shelves in stores were bare, food became almost unobtainable in the cities; in 1972 housewives marched in hunger demonstrations, in 1973 Chilean miners, the nation's most critical labour force, went on strike. Clothing, petrol, meat, nearly all the basic essentials, were in serious short-supply.

President Allende nationalised foreign holdings, including Chile's great copper mines, and what followed was a very real disaster; appeals for foreign loans, any kind of aid from the outside, were of course doomed.

Chile's previous production levels dropped. Her copper exports, the nation's foremost source of foreign exchange and credit, fell drastically, and in world banking circles, where nationalisation was anathemetized no matter where it occurred, Chilean loan applications were ignored.

Allende's course did not vary. He nationalised banks, factories, farms, even small shops, in spite of the outcries, until Chile's military – already alienated by Allende's importation of leftist terrorists from Cuba and elsewhere, by his bald-faced support of the Tupamaros in Uruguay, and by his avowed goal of communising the country – secretly met in crisis session, coordinated the efforts of all branches, then struck with a fury not only unprecedented in Chilean history, but unprecedented in recent Latin-American history. Terrorists were rounded up by the score. Some were accorded military trials before being shot. Others, with known terrorist affiliations, were shot on sight or were imprisoned.

Leftists fought back, from factories, alleys, rooftops, even from speeding cars, and small boats off the coast. Santiago, a city of almost 3 million people, became a battleground. Although the most prominent leftist leaders fled the country, many of their Chilean and foreign followers remained behind, unwilling or unable to flee.

Of the foreigners, many were refugees from the Tupamaro failure in nearby Uruguay. They were experienced urban guerillas. For a week there was a major battle between these opposing forces every day, and at night terrorists fanned-out robbing, murdering, and looting. The fall of Allende and his improbable dream engulfed Chile in the worst internal struggle of its recent history.

Because Chile's armed forces were traditionally separate from its civilian governments, by particular and deliberate design, when the armed-forces *junta* assumed control of the nation, almost no one outside the country knew anything about the new leaders. One of them, Police Commander Cesar Mendoza Duran, it was recalled when the names were published, had won an equestrian silver medal at the Helsinki Olympics in 1952, but that was about as far removed from being the participant in a bloody *coup* as could be imagined, so it did not help much in assessing Chile's new rulers.

Besides Commander Mendoza, there was the even less-known

commander of the Chilean air force, a suave, urbane general, Gustavo ("Gus") Leigh Guzman, and a hawknosed vice-admiral of Chile's quite modern navy, Jose Toribio Merino Castro, but the real strongman was Chile's top army officer, General Augusto Pinochet Ugarte, a burly, physically powerful man — like all the others, in his fifties — who was not a typical hard-fisted militarist, although in appearance he could have been.

Pinochet was a scholar, a sometime tactics and science instructor in his homeland, as well as in Ecuador, and the author of a number of books, which detailed incisive, and in-depth studies, of geography. Until Tuesday, 18th September 1973, the day of the fatal *coup* against Salvador Allende, Augusto Pinochet was not involved in politics. He was thought to be a progressive moderate — whatever that is — but he did not publicly express political opinions, and even those who knew Pinochet best, called him simply a nationalist or a centralist.

The centrifugal force which projected Augusto Pinochet and his three companions into political prominence was Chile's worsening economic situation, and the presence in the wings of hundreds of leftist revolutionaries at the head of thousands of armed, trained terrorists, awaiting the precise moment to attempt, with leftist backing from foreign powers, the same kind of a take-over which had come so perilously close to succeeding elsewhere, most notably in Uruguay, Jordan and Egypt.

Chile's *junta* profited from the lessons to be learned from Allende's procrastination. At the same time it moved tanks and troops into key positions throughout the country, and launched a deadly air and artillery attack upon La Moneda, with Salvador Allende inside at his desk, it undertook a vigorous round-up of all known terrorists, *barbudos*, leftists, and their sympathisers, and simultaneously sent special units to the schools, universities, even book stores, to confiscate and burn all the writings that could be found — by Mao, Marcuse, Marx, and Chile's own special socio-political theoretician and poet, Pablo Neruda, a Nobel Prize-winner.

Neruda had very recently died of cancer, otherwise he might not have fared too well as the *junta* deported terrorists by the hundreds, shot those taken in arms, imprisoned hundreds of others, and very efficiently eliminated every visible trace of leftism.

Chile's 10 million people, already in chaos, were abruptly also in terror. But the bloodletting, while certainly not minimal, rarely and only accidentally or inadvertently, touched the average Chilean. The leftist press cried out against 'thousands' of executions, and it was not incorrect. Santiago's nearly 3-million population suffered a loss — by body-count at the city morgue — of 2,796 corpses. The total national population of 10 million was lessened by an estimate of not less than 5,000 dead. This was not an exorbitant number of fatalities, either for a national population of 10 million, or for the number of known terrorists extant in Chile subsequent to the flight of hundreds from Uruguay after the Tupamaro debacle, or in view of Allende's 3-year period of sanctuary and asylum for terrorists from all over the world — unless, of course, you happened to be one of those fatalities.

The rightist purge continued. University instructors of suspected or known leftist sympathies were summarily ousted. Chile's *poblaciones* (ghettos) — slum districts, where Allende's staunchest supporters resided, and also the hotbeds of organised terrorism — became shambles after the soldiers passed through, and of course there were innocent victims, and atrocities as well, on both sides.

Censorship was imposed, legal rights were set aside, outside protests were blandly ignored, bands of roving youths bent on looting and theft were executed as leftists, confusion and fear spread, and the *junta*, while assuring the nation its freedom would shortly be restored, was in the position of the fire brigade that had stood by watching the flames spread until it was almost too late to put them out except by fighting fire with a greater fire. And in Chile, as in other lands, the foremost casualty — regardless of which side triumphed — was individual independence, with the second most critical injury accruing to the economy, left in ruin by Allende; so that regardless of the *junta's* best intentions, in late 1973 it took 7,000 Chilean escudos to equal 5 United States dollars. This was a condition that could not be speedily remedied even in a well-endowed country, but which, in a nation like Chile, could not possibly be corrected within a generation, if then, without large infusions of foreign aid and cash.

The cost of coddling terrorists has always been high. Too high for small nations to bear, and too expensive for wealthy nations to support. Rightism's answer has not, to date, been the correct alternative, but so far it has been the only answer that has sufficed in places such as Chile.

FOURTEEN

The Politics Of Confusion

Chile has not been the only example, but it has been a fairly recent one, and certainly a vivid one, of the bizarre over-lapping of criminality and terrorism. In former decades such crimes as abduction, bank-robbery, car-theft, and murder, were rationalised by both policemen and the average citizen as forms of felonious criminality. Al Capone, John Dillinger, Bonnie and Clyde, were criminals. Their motivation was fundamentally to acquire money illegally. Not one of them knew, except in a very vague way, where Beirut or Santiago or Amman was, and cared even less where they were.

Until fairly recent times a murder victim had relevance to his killer. Excluding hired assassins, and they were always a relatively insignificant minority, murderers had personal reasons for killing people, exactly as burglars had personal reasons for robbing affluent-appearing residences and business establishments. The criminal of the 'roaring 'twenties' and 'thirties, when individualised crime was nearing some kind of apex, was basically an entrepreneur, a self-employed, personally-motivated thief or killer. He performed his felonies for plain profit. He did not vote, did not belong to political parties, did not care about nor understand economics, and rarely had any ethnic or national feelings of any kind. Like the roving street gangs in beleaguered Santiago at the height of the Chilean backlash, he was simply an amoral opportunist willing to profit, if he could, despite the risk, from a situation he felt detached from and indifferent about. He was simply a criminal.

No one robbed banks in the 'twenties and 'thirties for ideological reasons. Extortionists did not hold hostages for ransom except to get if they could, and keep, the ransom. Armed men did not waylay truck convoys nor diplomatic limousines and either shoot their occupants or hurry them to a hideaway as a means of political protest.

Until fairly recent times criminals were as likely to be interested in profit as were legitimate businessmen, and as legitimate businessmen still are; but evidently as part of the evolving socio-political ethos, fresh, or perhaps latent, tendencies, have in relatively recent times, relegated the traditional criminal to a position of mundane status, and the newer variety of lawbreaker whose unique actions demonstrate the fresher tendencies, has become not only more numerous, but has also become more difficult to understand, and more deadly.

Further, this comparatively recent addition to the criminal hierarchy has defied specific categorisation, which was seldom the case with oldtime bankrobbers, car-thieves, purse-snatchers, or burglars. His motives have rarely been the same as those of the ordinary profit-motivated lawbreaker. In fact, as in the case of that Chicago organisation, 'De Mau Mau' — although the police had a number of murder victims, because they could imagine no motives, they could not match the crimes to specific criminals. By applying oldtime detection techniques, which were based entirely upon a criminal having a personal reason for committing his crime, they probably never would have resolved all those wanton slayings, unless, as occurred, an informant came forward.

The new terrorist could not be defined by the oldtime definitions. He was far less amenable to explanation by the developed schemata, which could quite often predict with a fair degree of success, when and where an ordinary, commonplace criminal would strike. His motives were not always rational and quite generally they most certainly lacked the fundamental practicality of, say, the professional hold-up man, or 'mugger'.

Most critical of all, the police, as in the 'De Mau Mau' affair, lagged far behind in recognising that this new variety of felon required up-dated approaches to the less traditional, more innovative, newer techniques and motivations.

The average citizen, with less reason to assess correctly and comprehend, had to view the new variety of criminal with even more bewilderment. Whatever became of the daring half-hero, the 'cat-burglar' who devised a way to climb sheer brick walls in order to burgle high-rise apartments, or the clever bank-robber, a master of disguises, who ran his course until tracked down by routine police work, and who, Robin Hood-like, left clever notes behind, capturing the popular fancy? Or what became of the money-motivated mobsters, the Capones, Dillingers, the Mafia-hierarchists?

Even Henri Landru, France's notorious mass-murderer of women he courted for their money, and who was executed in 1922, was understandable; these deplorable people with their motivations of personal gain, as simultaneously repellent and fascinating as they were, fit into a typical pattern. Their ingenuity, which quite often was brilliant, they used essentially for profit. They were traditionalists.

The other 'traditionalists', the police, as well as the average citizen, were comfortable in their belief that criminals would inevitably succumb to the accrued detection and apprehension techniques. Then came the terrorist. He did not usually fit the pattern, except in the sense that he violated laws. He harmed, killed, and destroyed with a great degree of personal detachment. As in the case of the Japanese gunman in the Israeli airport who sprayed bullets killing people he had never seen before, the fact that he survived that affair to be classified as a murderer only categorised his crime. It did not really help the average person to understand why even a zealot would indiscriminately kill human beings, such as the Puerto Rican pilgrims who fell before his gunfire, who had absolutely nothing at all to do with his avowed pro-revolutionary pan-Arabism.

For the average person this kind of a crime was baffling. It could not really be explained as a political act. When Gavrilo Princip assassinated Austria's archduke at Sarajevo in 1914, he committed a political killing. When a small Arab named Sirhan Bishara Sirhan killed Robert Kennedy, the pro-Israeli brother of a late United States President, he committed an act of political murder. These things were understandable. Even the murder of Israeli athletes at the XX Olympiad in Germany in 1972, was a comprehensible act of political violence, but how could the wanton slaying at the Israeli Airport be explained? Insanity — maniacal blood-lust? Psychiatrists who exhaustively examined the Japanese gunman certified him absolutely sane and rational.

Terrorists have plundered bank vaults, using identical techniques for gaining access to those which the oldtime bank-robbers used. They stole fortunes without keeping a penny of it. They rarely hijacked aircraft for personal gain either, nor broke a dozen laws annually to commit acts of terrorism for personal gain. Although in time they became neither rare nor unique, and gradually compelled a conviction among police and laymen alike, that they were not traditionalists, for decades people either tried unsuccessfully to force them to fit traditional patterns, or else, as with the average person, they viewed the rise and spread of terrorism — with its commonplace blending of criminality, idealism and politics — as a confusing and largely inexplicable phenomenon.

Crimes, such as bombings, whose motivation in earlier times were somewhat limited, increased tremendously within a twenty-year period, roughly from 1950 to 1970. Terrorist murders and such incomprehensible affairs as the massacre of innocent people at the Israeli Airport by an undersized Japanese gunman, only happened in earlier decades once in a long while, and were invariably assumed to be the work of madmen, which most, in fact, were. Seemingly irrational crimes increased bewilderingly. Men and women terrorists literally threw their lives away in the most casual sacrifice. The newspaper-reading public noted that in one way or another politics were involved. Not especially commendable, nor even very rational politics in many cases but nevertheless where the oldtime profit-motive had once existed, there was subsequently a quite different motivation, and people could not shrug off dozens of aircraft exploding in mid-air, killing all aboard because a terrorist had sent a satchel-charge aboard, any more than they could dismiss an abduction whose culmination did not result in the abductors acquiring a fortune in unlisted banknotes, but resulted in perhaps a dozen imprisoned terrorists being freed in exchange for the abductee's life.

Politics and the new breed of international felon evidently went hand in hand. For the average person, groping for comprehension, it was an era for the politics of confusion, an era of the criminality of homogeneity, when crime and idealism and politics formed an unanalysable motivation for the dispassionate, almost detached, deadliness of the new breed. An entire new gestatory era had been under way and scarcely anyone knew it. The generic name was terrorist. The genesis had something to do with the Second World War and the decline of old orders and old myths. It also had much to do with twenty years of political illogic expounded from thousands of academic lecterns by faulty theoreticians less prominent than Leon Trotsky or Salvador Allende, but infinitely more successful at creating a class of new criminals, the terrorists They were programmed by the thousands, to react anarchically to whatever they had learned to oppose. Millions of emotionally unfit but physically mature young people entered Universities every year, were sifted, sorted and bundled, were 'academically adjusted' to specific curricula, and between two and four years later were dumped off the assembly line completely programmed to computer-like responses; they looked normal, seemed normal, could pass almost anywhere as being normal, but they had a dream-quality idealistic implant which enabled them to do things average people reacted to in bewilderment, and the old criminal classifications simply did not fit them.

In the United States a few years ago a man known only as 'D.B. Cooper' commandeered an aircraft in flight, was given a large sum of money to desist, parachuted to safety, presumably over the woodlands of the Pacific Northwest, and subsequently was never heard of again. Robin Hood had returned. Childe Harold had exchanged his palfry for an airliner, his saddle for a parachute seat-pack. The relief throughout North America was widespread and vociferous. 'D.B. Cooper' had re-instated the olden legend; a half-hero could still exist in these complex times, the myth was, after all, alive and well.

Throughout the United States a 'D.B. Cooper' cult emerged; the unknown criminal's alias began appearing everywhere. It was comforting to have, if only for a moment, a return to understandable rationality. As the years passed and no apprehension was made, frank comment at all levels of the United States society implied the hope that 'D.B. Cooper' never would be found. (To date he has not been.) Heaven forbid that any figurative Sheriff of Nottingham should succeed, because, within days of the 'D.B. Cooper' episode, other aircraft hijackers were wantonly and irresponsibly killing innocent air travellers again, for reasons that did not make sense to the admirers of Childe Harold. The bitter realities closed in again obscuring America's winged Robin Hood; the programmed new breed of criminals were multiplying with frightening speed, were creating international terrorist associations, were actually making sophisticated war against law and order and were becoming strong enough to challenge sovereign nations.

In the wake of 'D.B. Cooper's' brief notoriety, which was a refreshing flashback, the people who understood the least, had to accept as completely valid the terrifying actuality of an entirely new epoch of criminality, and collectively as a society, they did not understand it, nor know precisely what to do about it, and meanwhile the terror proliferated. No more than two or three armed men could invade national embassies to terrorise or murder the occupants, and could afterwards compel national governments to guarantee their safe flight to sanctuaries. A squad of men could take over government buildings and proclaim their philosophy of illogic to 100 million television spectators, and demand escorted motorcades to friendly or neutral territories.

National leaders as well as academicians confusedly classified terrorism of these kinds as legitimate dissent; they were as baffled as was the average man on the street. News media proclaimed the new criminality as the 'politics of dissent' and therefore entitled to toleration. Political assassination was not classified as murder except insofar as it was an act of killing. Political assassins became 'special' people, not accountable to the old laws concerned with murder.

Society, in the past, made a particular issue of the low living standards of criminals, as, if not an excuse for their crimes, then as a supportive reason for them, and without question in earlier eras this was largely valid; but latter-day terrorist criminality as a defiant response to poverty or even ethnic discrimination, was not valid.

Tarred and feathered by the I.R.A., a man stands tied to a Belfast lamp-post at 5 o'clock on a November morning, 1971

Devastation caused by a
Protestant terrorist bomb in
Belfast, October 1971

A member of the Ulster
Volunteer Force holding a
Japanese Armalite rifle

Unemployment, low living standards, all the social ills which such men as Thomas Edison, Henry Ford, Samuel Coleridge, even Aristotle and Galileo managed to survive without becoming activists, were no explanation, simply because most terrorists from affluent societies never experienced any of these things, and that fairly well destroyed another of society's comfortable old shibboleths. A university graduate whose academic finances were adequate, and to whom society offered employment and social acceptance, failed to fit the old format here, too. Even the ragged *Fedayeen* whose fanaticism was all the reason he needed to become a terrorist, did have alternatives, but he was not programmed to accept them.

The reason for terrorism's proliferation lay elsewhere. The vast majority of people recognised this much, although they could not quite rationalise why the responses had to be so irrationally deadly; and when it might be suggested that terrorism throughout the world was an outgrowth of too much prosperity and too little of a need for actual labour for existence, that would not meet with a very general acceptance either.

Education, people have always correctly believed, was the answer to society's many and varied ills, and yet the majority of terrorism's most notorious leaders have been the products of accredited academic institutions; they have been the devisers of nihilist systems which by and large have not been concerned with change or improvement, but have been systematically and totally disruptive and destructive. Those who have been educated have not been favourable to education for others, or for re-education for their enemies. They have demonstrated time and again that what education means to them is the saturation of minds with propaganda; a novice terrorist must never be allowed to reflect upon things which oppose his system, he must believe whole-heartedly, that whatever stands in opposition to the things he believes in, must be destroyed. That has been all education has ever meant to the leaders of terrorism's expanding hierarchies. Here again, society has come face to face with a dilemma; its sons and daughters have returned from academia as programmed revolutionaries. If not terrorists in actuality, they form, by and large, as sympathisers, as facile, manipulatable robots, something else society has not recognised as yet because it has not been triggered to act — an entire and enormous preponderance of humanity, intellectually computerised to act on a signal in the interests of nihilism.

FIFTEEN

A New Force

Since the Second World War no regional map has been so amenable to alteration as has been the case of maps of the Middle East. Beginning with the United Nations 1947 plan of partition, and concluding with the 1973 so-called 'Yom-Kippur War', there have been four distinct changes, each one of benefit to the State of Israel at the expense of Israel's Arab neighbours. During the period of fraught *detente* between wars, there was no peace for either side, and very patently there would be no peace — whether Israel yielded up part or all the territories she acquired in 25 years of armed confrontation and conflict, or whether she did not.

Still, custom and tradition prevailed in late 1973, Israel and her enemies, the aligned Arab nations, met at Geneva's *Palais des Nations* for still another, and the latest, of their recurring peace conferences, and as before, each side could bargain from a posture of power, not as a result of the 1973 war even though both the Israelis and the Arabs had achieved gains, but because each antagonist sat in the shadow of a super power.

This of course was not novel; the Soviet Union had been supporting its Arab allies for years, exactly as the United States had been supporting the Israelis. What was novel at Geneva during the 1973 peace discussions, was that for the first time in the *Palais des Nations*, terrorists sat as accredited negotiators.

Up, until 1973 terrorism, considered a variety of world-wide criminality, had sent its representatives to arbitrate at the jungle-tent level on practically every continent, but genuine, recognised and orthodox negotiations have consistently been the obligation of accredited, official, and usually politically orthodox, leaders. So, at the *Palais des Nations*, everything followed time-hallowed custom; protocol was strictly observed, the polemics were predictable — the foreign ministers of Jordan and Egypt accused the Israelis of mass-murder, unprovoked aggression, and terrorism, while Israel's Abba Eban accused the Arabs of having the "mentality and ideology that produced the gas chambers . . . of Auschwitz". Nearby were terrorist leaders in the role of respectable negotiators, as representatives of a new world force which was not bound by the national, regional, or ethical concept which to a more or less degree, governed the actions and the rhetoric of other negotiators.

While the orthodox representatives strove to reach a balance, if not a genuine accord, and while their orthodox armies were — more or less — observing a cease-fire, the forces of terror were acting in their customary manner, which was not orthodox by most standards, although by every standard of terrorism, these things *were* orthodox, the basic operational principle of terrorism being simply to function outside established rules, customs and laws.

Not even the capitulation discussions which concluded the Second World War were as completely engulfed in security measures as were the 1973 Israeli-Arab conferences. Fear of terrorists obsessed the hapless Swiss, with good reason. They escorted peace delegates to their hotels under stiflingly oppressive motorised units of security police, on the ground, while overhead police helicopters hovered low. The Israeli hotel, La Reserve, was converted into a fortress with extremely elaborate security measures being taken not only within the hotel itself, but also in adjoining buildings and even in the air space above.

The atmosphere in Geneva appeared to be a composite of fear and hope — mostly fear. Whether the talks produced anything satisfactory or not, the longer they went on the more real became the nightmare-possibility of a terrorist attack.

In fact, there was an atttack, but not in Geneva, and those who chose, for whatever reason, to make a claim of disassociation between this attack and the Geneva conference had to admit two facts which were clearly apparent; one, the terrorists were Arab dissidents, two, they did not in all probability plan their act of terrorism without full knowledge of the repercussions it would have in Geneva.

The attack occurred at Rome's Leonardo da Vinci airport in mid-September 1973, when the Geneva delegates were preparing to meet in an atmosphere of super-charged tension.

Following the custom of others who have launched similar attacks, five men, all Palestinian Arabs, appeared in the thronged airport armed with grenades, submachine guns and automatic pistols, and without warning began firing.

People ran in panic, the terrorists rounded up a number of Italian airport security officers, along with several other people, took them outside to the flight line where a number of aircraft were boarding passengers, and hurled phosphorus bombs through the doors of a Pan American airliner. When the bombs detonated, tearing holes in the aircraft and filling its interior with flames, several passengers managed to tumble out. Others, trapped inside, could be heard screaming over the roar of flames. Thirty people were incinerated.

The terrorists then boarded a Lufthansa airliner, and as though to impress the pilot, when an Italian ground-crew maintenance man turned away, a terrorist shot him point-blank in the back, adding one more fatality.

The Lufthansa aircraft pilot was ordered by the terrorists to fly them and their hostages to Athens, which he did. There, the aircraft was cleared to land, but when the terrorists demanded that the Greek authorities release two Arab terrorists in their custody, the Greeks refused, and the terrorists then shot and killed one of their Italian hostages, an airport worker from Rome named Ippolito.

The aircraft then flew out of Athens and eventually landed in Kuwait where the terrorists — although mildly denounced by Kuwaiti officials, who could do little else in the face of the storm aroused in Europe over the savagery perpetrated in Rome — were ultimately allowed to go free.

The result of this affair was eighteen injured and thirty-one dead. It was classified as the "most horrifying single incident yet staged" by terrorists, but in fact other, prior terrorist attacks in both the Middle East and Latin America had resulted in more havoc, destruction of property, and death.

But none cast the pall over the peace talks at Geneva's *Palais des Nations* that this one did, nor were the Israelis allowed to forget that something similar could engulf them at any moment. Among the entourages of their adversaries in Geneva were the known leaders of terrorist bands. And even assuming, as both the Israelis and their Swiss hosts had to do, that terrorists would not strike while their countrymen were nearby and liable to injury from counter-action, was not a very safe course. Of the thirty victims who perished in the Pan American aircraft at Leonardo de Vinci airport in Rome, four had been Arab officials of the Moroccan government.

Also, the expertise of seasoned terrorists had progressed a very long way since Gavrilo Princip's assassination of an Austrian archduke back in 1914. It had become entirely feasible to kill a high official of state, such as Luis Carrero Blanco, Premier of Spain, with practically no peril of apprehension, and to do it in such a manner that both police and intelligence officials confessed to being impressed by the assassination technique.

Carrero Blanco's slayers were reminiscent of Latin-America's Tupamaros. They rented a cellar adjoining the street used by Carrero Blanco in his daily trip from the church of San Francisco de Borja, where he attended mass, to his Madrid office. With considerable skill they painstakingly spent two months tunneling from their cellar to the centre of the roadway, shoring up the overhead pavement with steel supports as they advanced the full forty-five feet. In the centre of the roadway, they created two separate segments paralleling the main tunnel, all three pointing in the direction from which the Premier's chauffeur-driven vehicle would approach.

Three individual explosive charges were placed, one in each tunnel. These were wired in circuit to a safely-distant observation point. Every precaution was taken. For example, to preclude a delayed, or a premature, detonation, a red line was marked upon the wall opposite, where Carrero Blanco's car would line up in this 'sight', and when it did, Premier Carrero Blanco's undeviating morning regimen brought him to his death.

The black car containing Carrero Blanco and his chauffeur was hurled five storeys high in the air on a slanting trajectory which carried it over the church's rectory roof to a balcony on the far side where it came to rest upon its side.

The explosion created a hole in the street six feet deep and about twenty feet in diameter. Adjacent buildings sustained damage and other cars parked nearby were demolished. Uniquely, no other people were killed.

Experienced observers were impressed by the meticulous preparations as well as by the sophisticated expertise of the terrorists. Those who were awed at the force of the explosive, all other things considered, were left with no doubt but that the slayers of Spain's Premier had absolutely no intention of having their victim survive.

Conjecture immediately placed blame for Carrero Blanco's death at the hands of the communists, which was a reasonable assumption, Carrero Blanco being a lifelong anti-communist. But there were also Basque separatists, a very violent and capable people. There were also embittered Asturian miners, as well as a number of splinter left-wing groups with private axes to grind who could have been responsible. The government seemed to favour placing blame on the Basque separatists, but the point was, once a premier of Spain, or any other country, had been assassinated, and the matter of recovery had been attended to, the terrorists were still there; they could still reach a premier – or totally unsuspecting people boarding an airliner in Rome, or a foreign minister of Israel whether he appeared in Rome or Tel Aviv.

Terrorism as a force, whether lent respectability by having its representatives accredited to the prestigious *Palais des Nations* or not, continued to function as it customarily had, and its quite considerable knowledge of terror and terror tactics, were available to disgruntled Asturian miners, Basque separatists, or almost any other disruptive segment feeling a need for polarising attention. Terror tactics were indisputably designed to accomplish that; in fact, as with the catapulting of Luis Carrero Blanco into eternity, or somewhere anyway, the most spectacular acts of terrorism could be counted upon to bring immediate claims of responsibility. Sometimes there were as many as three or four such claims for an individual act. Carrero Blanco's death was at once claimed by Basques as their particular accomplishment.

Nor has refusing to recognise terrorism's leaders been very successful. At the *Palais des Nations* discussions, although both the

United States and the U.S.S.R. declined to permit Yassar Arafat's Palestine Liberation Organisation to actively participate at the initial round of conferences, in order to placate the Israelis — who were especially antagonistic towards Arafat's terrorist organisation — nevertheless there were representatives of the new force at every stage of the talks. Those Jordanian terrorist commandos who had so aroused the anger of Jordan's King Hussein three years prior to the Geneva talks that he had his army hunt them down and ostensibly stamp them out (at least in Jordan) subsequently appeared, quite alive and healthy, a part of the new force's political structure, as they always had been — their leaders demonstrating a fresh confidence, as well they might. The Arab unity arising from Arab so-called triumphs during and after the 1972 'Yom-Kippur War', sought to strengthen that unity by supporting Arafat against all others as official spokesman for the displaced Palestinians of the West Bank, that sector of land on Israel's side — the west side of the Jordan River — where roughly one million nearly destitute Arab refugees still reside in filth and squalor, a quarter of a century after being displaced by the Israelis.

How best to cope with these people was a dilemma no one, over a quarter of a century, was able to resolve, but Arafat and his Arab supporters in high office throughout such places as Egypt, Saudi Arabia, Lebanon and the U.S.S.R. looked with cautious approval at King Hussein's plan to create a separate, more or less autonomous state, out of the west-bank territory.

Israel was not at all pleased at the prospect of having still another Arab state on her borders. But the real manoeuvering would undoubtedly come from the unified Arabs. They could support the west bank plan, calling for the elimination of any Jordanian control, even police-patrolling activity. If Hussein demurred, since he had always been a foot-dragger in Arab causes and therefore had few genuine friends among the Arab states which bordered his country (and had even fewer friends in Israel) Arab unity could conceivably attack Jordan and overwhelm it in a matter of hours, before even those who, in the past, having demonstrated admiration for Hussein, could hasten to his aid.

The goal was the same as it had been three to five years earlier, when it appeared very likely to succeed — to take, not just the west bank, but all of Jordan for the new Palestinian state.

This move would placate alienated and resentful Arab leaders to whom King Hussein had been cast as a jackal. It would also enable Jordan to be over-run with practically no logistical problems, since the armed might of the belligerent Arab nations were still at hand, marking time until the outcome of the Geneva peace talks brought them back to war, or sent them home to be demobilised. Finally, if the Palestinians did have a national identity, almost the full length of Israel, across the Jordan River, the same ideology which had encouraged them to make their former bid to control Jordan, would certainly not be found to have atrophied through the interim. This was especially the case since Arab morale, particularly Palestinian or *Fedayeen* morale, had been allowed to soar to such extravagant heights after that shibboleth of Israeli invincibility had been so badly dented and dulled by events during the 'Yom-Kippur war'.

Arafat's terrorist organisation had high morale, finally. It also had something even more significant — a national character. Its allies were national powers, its recognition in the Middle East, and also in the Soviet Union, was grounded on nationalism. The P.L.O. might actually be only the same ragged organisation of dissidents, anarchists and perennially professional terrorists it had always been; but at the conclusion of the 'Yom-Kippur war' in 1973, there was no way to ignore the fact that, supported now by unified Arab strength, including the towering wealth and strategic power of Saudi Arabia's King Faisal, with one leader confirmed at the top, Yassar Arafat's P.L.O. could finally state without exaggerating, that the world would have to listen to the voice of those one million displaced Palestinians, who were in all probability going to finally become a nationality. The question to be answered was, obviously, just how much of Hussein's Hashemite kingdom might be carved up.

Another question worthy of consideration would have to do with what certainly would be in the minds of Israel's most adamant and implacable foes in Islam. Israel, bordered on her land sides by Lebanon, Syria, Saudi Arabia and Egypt, as well as by Jordan, has only been able to rely upon one of these Arab lands, Jordan, to procrastinate in times of confrontation. Providing that Jordan were to become the fifth knuckle of the Arab fist poised to smash Israel, an ally of the genuinely militant and stubbornly unyielding foeman of Israel, than by most scales of political calibration, even though it might not happen for five, ten, twenty, or perhaps even fifty years, it *would* happen; and Israel would be over-run.

There had to be some kind of demonstrable adaptability, though. Even the Soviet Union, more than half a century old in 1973, and imbued with some of the complacent stodginess of middle age, no longer actually as eager to rush into very many breaches manned by gaunt and disenfranchised zealots, as it once was, took a wary view of Arafat's terrorists, and offered tentative support providing that the new force would promise to do nothing which might destroy the Geneva peace conference. Arafat agreed, indicating that he, too, had achieved a plateau where respectability might actually be desirable — then P.L.O. terrorists struck. In the second week of September 1973, two terrorists incidents erupted which resulted in three dozen casualties. Elsewhere, there were other acts of terrorist violence. What the Kremlin's reaction was to all this could only be imagined, but for the new force, every act of successful terrorism added another mote to the growing, heady confidence; nor did the supporters of *jehad* in Islam do more than feign shock or dismay or horror, while actually they were known to have private havens ready and available for fleeing terrorists.

There simply was no way for anyone to guarantee that terrorists, in the Middle East, or almost anywhere else in the world, would not strike. Oaths to desist meant nothing. Emboldened by the Arab showing of strength and unity, Middle East terrorism increased steadily and rather spectacularly, subsequent to the 'Yom Kippur war'.

It had achieved the status of force and perhaps it would in time also achieve respectability; if it did it would then pass from the scene as other, earlier, associations of fanatics had also done.

As long as there is dissent — not exclusively in the Middle East but everywhere — there will also be terrorism, its victims not necessarily enemies of Islam or even averse to terrorism, just unfortunate enough to be where they should not have been when a terrorist indiscriminately opens fire or hurls his grenade.

One aspect of terrorism, the killing of totally disassociated, completely innocent bystanders, although it could invoke outrage in most orderly areas, had been done so many times that the indignation had begun to be a little forced. Who, for example, bothered to mention by name the unfortunate chauffeur who was driving Premier Luis Carrero Blanco's car down the Calle de Claudio Coello in Madrid at Christmas time of 1973, when both men were blown to bits?

SIXTEEN

Terrorism And Foreign Policy

Everyone — from those responsible for the making of national and international policy to the commonplace citizens at large in their stores, shops or factories — views the entire world from a private viewpoint, and reacts, as a result of that private viewpoint, to the policies and actions of foreigners.

Each individual, as well as each nation, and in fact each region within a nation, is unique inasmuch as each has its own interests, geography, and problems. Nations give priorities to their interests, as do individuals; for a nation the foremost concern is security, safety, proper and adequate defence. For an individual the foremost concern is also safety, but an individual interprets the term differently; his safety means full employment, health protection, a defence against the time when he can no longer work, assured wages, a roof that does not leak, adequate food, an opportunity for his children.

For the individual as for the nation, political change can amount to very real peril. The man employed in a shop sees the threat to his job — his entire personal, private world — the moment foreigners decide they will no longer provide the oil which lubricates the bearings in his car, or the fuel which fires the furnace in his home and shop.

The individual reacts. The nation reacts. People and nations react to all change, but their reactions to policies inaugurated by foreigners are almost without exception, in the initial stage, antagonistic. People distrust change. They fear it. Everyone views change from his particular point of reference — how it will affect his nation's economy, his nation's welfare and security. But essentially, the individual citizen becomes anxious over what change in the world means to him personally as an individual.

Few Japanese or Americans could view an Arab oil-boycott favourably, obviously, since it very clearly would not simply imperil their national economies — something even an American storekeeper or a Japanese fisherman could not help but understand — but more immediately and personally relevant, an Arab oil boycott would threaten their personal effort to survive. It would endanger jobs, opportunities, personal concerns and interests, family safety, and the individual efforts to survive.

All political change has to be grounded upon national or regional necessity, real or imaginary, upon the wide-ranging interests of nations or communities of nations. It must also be supported by some kind of force or power, and in a world where the preponderant factor of force is controlled by only two nations, two super powers, national foreign policy at the lesser level can only hope to achieve recognition and a degree of political equality — providing it can rattle a weapon of sufficient importance to gain the attention of the greater powers, which the lesser nations cannot begin to match in force.

Stated differently, all the small nations watched for a decade while United States force levelled mountains in South-east Asia, obliterated entire towns, cities, even forests, up-ended an agrarian economy and left it hanging in limbo. Whether such a nightmare were even a remote peril to, say, the terrorists adjacent to the Red Sea or the Gulf of Aden, did not change the clear fact that such force *did exist*, did impinge upon the Arab world's ranging interests, did, quite clearly, amount to change; and the Arab nations as well as individual Arabs had to face the same unpleasant prospect that the Japanese fisherman and the United States storekeeper had to face. Change imperilled both national and individual safety. It also appeared as a regional threat. The reaction, then, had to be defensive. The only force Kuwait and Saudi Arabia could advance to counter the power of United States force in their own geographical sphere, where Arab interests, values, and aspirations were imperilled by the octopus-like expansion of United States power, was simply the only weapon they possessed — oil.

There was risk. There has never been political change without risk. But the alternatives, as seen through Arab eyes, warranted the risk; a triumphant, flourishing Israel, supported and encouraged by a super power, in a part of the world where widespread enlightenment has been more generally retarded over the centuries than in almost any other area, had to be resisted. Change in the Middle East, political first, then social change, appeared to endanger not just Islam's way of life, but also Islam's territory. Arab leaders and policy-makers, regarding the industrialised, flourishing technologically-advanced establishment of Israel in their midst, were compelled to face the fact that if Israel were allowed to prosper, their own long-established regional leadership was most certainly going to be challenged, and possible usurped, which was a change they could not and would not countenance.

But that concerned only social change. The matter of territorial change was another matter, and regardless of the rhetoric of protest which went forth from both Washington and Tel Aviv after each Israeli-Arab confrontation, inundating Arab capitals with assurances that the United States-supported nation of Israel had no expansionist territorial aspirations, the plain facts proved otherwise. In 1947 Israel was a patchwork of fragile interdependencies. By 1949 these interdependencies had elbowed their way towards a unified nationalism by nibbling away at the adjacent Syrian, Lebanese and Jordanian territories. By 1967, Israel, having acquired the Sinai Peninsula, as well as additional Jordanian territory, was twice as large in land area as it had been originally, and in the areas of influence, regional force, and military power, it was a genuine threat to all its neighbours. By 1973, with more Arab territory acquired, well on its way to becoming the most aggressive military power in the Middle East, appearing as a very genuine peril to all its neighbours as well as to other more distant but equally as anxious Arab nations, some as distant as black Africa, the situation for each individual Arab, who constituted the equivalent of the United States storekeeper or the Japanese fisherman, was fundamentally the same as it was for those other two reluctant sharers of the same winds of political change. But, from the Arab's viewpoint, there was one difference — the peril by 1973, had become more than simply a possibility. When a super power, recently disengaged from Southeast Asia, turned in the direction of Islam and Israel, the threat which was inherent in this change evoked predictable reactions at all levels in Islam; defence required more than arms. Even with Soviet backing, Israel's neighbours could not really expect an armed confrontation to produce salutary results for a number of reasons. Nor could they expect to survive such a course of action, under Soviet aegis, without very possibly losing as much to their red imperialist ally, as they stood to lose to United States supported Israel.

The remaining alternative was to employ their own best weapon, keeping the Soviet Union at arms length, where possible, and still bringing sufficient pressure to bear upon the other super power, the United States, to accomplish, hopefully and at the very least, a stalemate.

Super powers, as well as small powers such as Israel — whose industrial and military force was greater than that of any Arab state, and whose mechanisation was also superior to the mechanisation of any Arab power — ran on oil. Saudi Arabia and Kuwait could not wage successful war against an adversary no larger than they were. Neither of them had a valid armed force. Indeed, they could not even wage war against an enemy smaller than they were, that was as industrialised and technologically advanced as was Israel. But they could confront such an adversary whose tanks, aircraft, munitions factories and sea-going ships could not function without oil, by denying Israel oil, and by also using oil as their weapon against Israel's ally — the most highly industrialised nation on earth, the United States.

This was the Arab world's reaction when a super power appeared in Islam casting a long shadow. For Islam leaders, policy makers and strategy planners, viewing the world from their particular points of reference, the clear course to be adopted as a reaction to unwelcome political change in their region, had to be defensive action, the same variety of indignant response to be encountered in the United States and other oil-boycotted nations, once the Arab response was felt.

Once the winds of political change have been set free, adversaries as well as allies tend to bend in the same direction, tend to do the same things in reaction, but for different reasons.

This carries right on down to the hermetic world of the Japanese fisherman, the United States storekeeper, and now also to the world of the Arab leather-worker. The reaction to change amounts to resistance. In former times this resistance usually resulted in fishing villages, small towns, and desert villages, being emptied of men. Armies marched. It was a healthy way of working off frustrations. Hazardous, admittedly, but then so was falling out of bed, or crossing a street in Damascus in mid-day, or looking left as one stepped off the sidewalk in London. But the dangers of marching had been increasing astronomically each year since the Second World War, which inaugurated the era of one bomber equalling half a million human beings. War might be desirable, even advantageous, but there could never again, after the Second World War, be a *safe* war. Those whose greatest appreciation of the hazards of war were, by 1973, the same great powers between whom a number of hair-raising confrontations had kept civilisation at the brink for a quarter of a century. By 1973 they were also the same two powers whose fragile *detente* fooled no one; they each had, and would use, a capability for devastation unprecedented in all history.

Under these circumstances, obviously, no rational man would actually seek war, and certainly neither of the super powers could *want* war. Men fight for a legion of reasons, but essentially they wage war to win. A peril which has been able to compound itself annually for twenty-five years, until its capacity to over-kill precludes victory for either side, has to be a deterrent, rather than an inspiration or an encouragement. But that does not negate the possibility of super powers being drawn into war, as could easily happen when the national communities which have been actively supported and supplied by the separate super powers, attack one another.

The era of the 'splendid little war' came and went. Every armed confrontation subsequent to 1945 sent people to bed all over the world with nightmares. The enormity of what subsequently portended dwarfed Damocles' sword to hatpin size. Whatever the outcome of regional clashes, the actual result had to be measured according to what could have happened.

Escaping the 'big bang' in a dozen different parts of the world from Cuba to Cambodia, from Uruguay to Ghana did not establish a pattern of avoidance, nor a precedent of preclusion, it instead increased the odds against additional escapes, by stiffening the resolve, on one side or the other, each time someone had to back down.

Regardless of how resentful the Japanese fisherman or the American storekeeper may have felt about an oil boycott, or how aggravated an Arab or an Israeli may have felt over battle casualties and national humiliations, at the level of leadership each reaction to change, to threats, to perils, had to be perceived and acted upon in the great shadow, not of what might ensue as the result of a Six-Day War, or even a Three-Weeks War, but of what undeniably would follow if the super powers were finally unable or unwilling to avoid the ultimate confrontation.

The prospects for peace have never been great, but following the Second World War the prospects for war had to diminish. If they did not the other, more awesome prospect had, over the years, to add its weight to the far greater hazard until rational leaders, regardless of zeal and even of provocation, would consider every overt action in the light of what they could quite possibly be unleashing — a wipeout.

For the super powers, this political quicksand was avoidable up to a point. Beyond that, they could be sucked into exactly what many of the world's knowledgeable minds have conceived of as being inevitable. Each aggravation, so the reasoning went, diminished the chances for peace. Each regional war, with a super power discernible in the background, favouring opposite belligerents, brought into sharper focus the incongruity of little nations making war over useless tracts of desert.

No thinking human being went to bed anywhere in the world when Israel launched her 1967 Six-Day-War, without knowing exactly what real fear was. In 1973 the war took longer and the results were less easy to define, but again, a coterie of relative indigents had edged the world closer to cataclysm over the same goals, and they were no better in 1973 than they had been in 1967, but they had lowered the odds one more numeral.

The fear of a future stopped short by a mushroom-cloud, a blinding flash of very pale light, and a deafening explosion that no one would hear, increasingly occupied leaders and planners. In the passing of time all but the most irresponsible people came to regard even small, contained wars, as anything but excusable, and the denial of this 'last right of kings', created a vacuum which could be filled by the employment of less time-hallowed instrument of foreign policy, *the professional terrorist*.

In former times mercenary soldiers provided a near approximation of terrorism. Men who waged war for pay alone reduced conflict to its lowest level. Throughout history the mercenary warrior, valorous though he may have been, consistently, by his behaviour on the field and off, brought little honour to his employer, and brought even less honour to the military profession. More recently, a tendency developed to adapt to altered times, which in turn were seemingly motivated by the antipathy towards small wars arising from the fear of those who made them, and those who observed them — that an error or a miscalculation could destroy all — winner, loser and observer.

Small wars, such as the Arab-Israel conflict of late 1973, the 'Yom-Kippur War', aroused rather general condemnation. Among even the opposing super powers there appeared to be only very reluctant encouragement of their respective and opposing embattled allies at levels above the military. To all others, spectators, observers, and even sympathisers, who could conceivably have been drawn in if the war had spread, the concensus appeared to be a rather unanimous condemnation, based, one may assume, on the valid logic that to risk unrestricted total war between the United States and the U.S.S.R. over a relatively worthless stretch of desert called Sinai, whether Moses received the Tablets atop a barren, ugly mountain there or not, was patently inconceivable and ridiculous.

All small wars were viewed as pointlessly risky; they could not be made popular even among their planners nor participants, therefore, since conflict had historically been, and still remained, the most effective lever of foreign policy, its ultimate tool, and it had become universally unpopular, the alternative was undeclared war, conflicts for which responsibility could be denied. Mercenaries could be hired, but not uniformed. Government support in arms and money — and sanctuary, but not always, obviously, since that betrayed the sponsor — could, and was, clandestinely supplied.

These hirelings, though, have not fitted the accepted classification of mercenary soldiers. They have been, in fact, terrorists.

Portugal, as an example, in her long conflict with rebelling African colonials, waged a savage and discreet war, rarely mentioned for many years, with minimal publicity, and with most of the actual devastation being undertaken by hired terrorists, sometimes referred to as guerillas, but who were men who owed loyalty to no man and no cause — who terrorised for cash.

Almost unknown outside of black Africa, these groups carried their unremitting variety of terrorism to the heartland of Portugal's colonial foes with terrible effect. One man, Daniel Francisco Roxo, a former white hunter in Mozambique, with a terrorist band of 90 black Africans, in less than a decade, caused the death by gunfire and bombs of more rebelling Frelimo (Front for the Liberation of Mozambique) insurrectionists, than had the entire Portuguese African expeditionary force of 60,000 national troops, and the national troops had aircraft, artillery, and even missiles.

Roxo's terrorists, known as the *Coluna Infernal*, or Column of Fire, knew their territory better than most native blacks knew it. They operated by stealth, extracted information and intelligence by torture, killed on sight, devastated at will, dispatched captives by the knife, and Roxo, called by the Frelimo, the 'Devil of Niassa', who was a physically powerful, bearded man, demonstrated his absolute mastery of terrorist techniques by simply staying alive while being the most hated white man in black Africa.

Roxo was an example of how aggressive national foreign policy could continue to function according to long-established precepts, without sponsoring a declared war. Portugal's position in Africa had been a matter of precarious balance for over ten years. Colonialism has been out of style for at least three times that long. A general war of suppression and attrition would have brought down upon Portugal the indignation of every nation, and very possibly the results of that indignation would have been sanctions against Portugal.

Besides the unpopularity of small wars, there was, in this case, the more prevalent and universal feeling of antipathy against colonialism. Portugal's alternatives were to either risk sanctions, and perhaps worse, active interference by outside sympathisers with the Frelimo rebels, or the employment of terrorists such as Roxo's *Coluna Infernal*, who were not national troops; were not in fact even mercenary guerillas, unless that categorisation were expanded to include terrorists who destroyed whatever they came upon, including the property of those they served, as well as those they hunted.

Roxo's variety of terrorists have functioned in accordance with the handbooks on terrorism written in Moscow, Peking and Havana, but they did so as an extenuation of Portuguese foreign policy.

They appeared in the same nondescript camouflaged jungle attire worn by their Frelimo foemen. Like Vietnamese terrorists, they did not wage war, they practised terrorism, and the ultimate probability of Daniel Francisco Roxo appearing elsewhere, outside of Africa, should he survive, is very likely — is, in fact to be expected. Roxo's kind of terrorism has always been greatly in demand. In the future, with terrorism gaining acceptance among the foreign offices of the world as the best available alternative to small wars, men such as Roxo will, somehow or other, be made to appear respectable.

The only link between Roxo's kind of terrorism, and mercenary soldiers, is that both are for hire. But even that distinction may be fast disappearing, for although, quite generally, terrorists, have been motivated by ideology, or pure nihilism, many instances in Ireland, Canada, the Middle East and Latin America have appeared, demonstrating that terrorists can be hired for cash.

Terrorism, then, having perfected its techniques, having established a loose, world-wide confederation, having become an accepted element of foreign policy, and having achieved international accreditation at Geneva, being represented at the high councils of many nations, where it has become the suitable alternative to brush-fire wars in the last third of the twentieth century has earned the distinction of being considered desirable even by those who formerly denounced it the loudest.

SEVENTEEN

Terrorism's Third Way

It has been said that politics feeds on vacuums. So also, one may assume, does dissent.

Terrorism flourishes where politics and dissent create vacuums, but it has not been limited to a singular nor a specific spawning ground; it also appears, at times, to create its own sponsoring environment. It seems to be endemic. It appears where there is a void, a thralldom, it appears where there is tumult, agitation and dissent, and it also appears in advance of any of these circumstances, bringing its own environment with it.

If these facts have been suggestive of an inevitability, they may also have implied that terrorism is predictable, which it has been, more so in some cases than in others. Terrorists fade and revive, they adopt protective colouration and they abandon it; but they remain essentially predictable.

For example, while the Hashemite army of Jordan's King Hussein waged an unrelenting campaign against *Fedayeen* terrorists in Jordan during the early 'seventies, with results which were announced through the press to a hopeful world as being quite satisfactory, as a matter of fact the terrorists were never more than inconvenienced, and the moment it became advantageous for them to re-appear in Jordan and elsewhere, while preparations were under way for the 1973 attack upon Israel, they augmented the climate of agitation and dissent; they then predictably appeared in the midst of it, as strong and resolute as ever.

To predict the arrival of terrorism, all that was required was the knowledge that a variable but basically consistent set of circumstances existed. Where there existed a faltering or inflationary economy, a war-devastated area, a vacuum of destitution, in short, where there existed economic, political, moral and spiritual procrastination, terrorism spawned.

In a void of ferment, turmoil, demoralisation, terrorism provided a way to survive which fed upon the accumulation of financial fat stored in the body politic during epochs of orderly growth. It did so in order to abet the destruction of systems which it despised, rarely with any genuine alternate system in mind.

Terrorism's third way was to destroy the system, regardless of its variety. The triumph, if there was to be one, was to be a triumph of nihilism; survival was to be ensured through the acquisition of all substance, which was to be exploited, not re-established nor re-ordered. Terrorism's fundamental law has consistently been that of the jungle: take by force what has been naturally provided.

In cases where terrorism had to provide a system, as among Uruguay's Tupamaros, its basic law remained consistent. It was still jungle law. If exigencies required rules, they came down from the top as the most primitive kind — obey or perish. There were more laws inciting death than laws preserving life. Become old, feeble, or ill, and be punished by being slain. Seek something better than nihilism and be rewarded as an enemy of terrorism, for which the penalty was death. Fail at any undertaking, at any level, and expect execution. Achieve excellence as a nihilist, and risk being slain for superior capabilities.

As a political malignancy, the third way steadily consumed its host. Given a nation of its own, in Jordan, in Chile, in Africa, or anywhere at all, terrorism would at once begin to feed upon its neighbours because it cannot create, it can only consume. Legitimise terror, through a tolerant political ambience, and watch the cancerous spread of its nihilistic appetite.

In the final months of 1972 when the United States and North Vietnamese peace negotiators roughed in the terms by which a disillusioned Childe Harold — the United States — could abandon Vietnam, President Nixon's chief negotiator, Henry Kissinger, in referring to the peace terms stated that it seemed quite clear that "whether this agreement brings a lasting peace or not depends not only on its provisions but on the spirit in which it is implemented", and subsequently both Henry Kissinger and the United States withdrew, which the north had never made any secret about being its sole reason for negotiating; and that had nothing to do with peace, only with getting rid of a troublesome interloper who had managed to bring pressure on Hanoi from both Moscow and Peking. Without the interloper on hand, Peking and Moscow could return to their earlier support of the north, and the north could re-organise and re-energise its policy of devastation and terrorism in the south.

Never at any time did North Vietnam intend to de-escalate the war, and as the prospects for victory became increasingly less substantial, more diaphanous and tenuous, the more free rein and support North Vietnam gave to every variety of terrorism in the south, encouraging destruction and devastation for their own sakes. What could not quite be conquered, then, should be subjected to the third way; terrorists should be encouraged to destroy, consume, pollute, lay waste.

Since the cease-fire accord the rate of ruin has not diminished. Nor has the rate of dying. But terrorism has escalated, both in the countryside and in the cities, all of it with the tacit approval of both adversaries, Hanoi and Saigon. A century ago the same condition existed in Mexico, where great armed hosts made an almost unnoticed metamorphosis from partisan armies to swarming terrorist legions whose vision extended no further than the front sight of their gunbarrels. They straggled through the red haze of a hundred burning cities, locust-like consuming everything in their path, completely unwilling to see that what they were destroying was their land. They were also un-caring – pure nihilists.

Terrorism is not just spawned in decay, social, political, moral and spiritual decay, but it certainly proliferates better if those elements are present, and they are always present, even during eras of affluence; they are, in fact, endemic in every culture and in every civilisation, and where they appear, predictably, so will terrorism. There is a nexus, but thus far there has been little recognition of this fact, and even less provision made for safeguards, remedies or countermeasures.

The third way serves man. When United-Nations Secretary

General Kurt Waldheim opted for action against international terrorism in 1972, the African bloc nations, 41 strong, came out of executive session in September and blocked Waldheim's hopes for a general debate on ways to combat terrorism. Subsequently, the General Assembly's central political committee then voted to suspend the issue. The motion of suspension was made by Ambassador Radha Krishna Ramphal of Mauritius.

There remained a weak chance, even then, for consideration of the issue, providing the steering committee pressed a recommendation for debate. It did not press the issue, and the General Assembly shelved it.

The African-bloc nations had reasons for undermining any hope of establishing some form of control. Africa has been a continent in turmoil since the Second World War sponsored the advent of large-scale independence, and terrorism, which accompanied much of Africa's nationalism, lingered on long after most of the birth-pains had ended, a tool of value to unarmed or poorly armed black African states, for either internal or external use.

In Africa, personality cults such as the one created around Zaire's President Mobuta, arose out of savagery and bloodshed, pure terrorism. These establishments have been perpetuated the same way – by terrorism. In Zaire, wild, extravagant spending aroused fear among educated and responsible Zairois. When protests were made that Mobutu's government was spending money faster than it could be earned within the country, or borrowed outside Zaire, terrorists went after the protestors. Throughout black Africa terrorism as a tool of both internal and external policy has been used with greater indulgence than anywhere else in the world during recent times. One African nation a few years ago undertook through a policy of extermination and absolute terrorism to destroy an entire tribe called Ibo, within its own borders.

African tribalism and terrorism have long been compatible. Some knowledgeable Africans have viewed them as being almost synonomous. Any threat to limit or outlaw terrorism had to find disfavour among the United Nations' African bloc. The third way, in the most recently enfranchised part of the world, had a long and accepted history.

But there could have never been much hope, even without the black-bloc vote against a United Nations debate on terrorism, that any such debate could have taken place, and certainly if such a debate had taken place, it could not have resulted in sanctions or restrictions. Terrorism, in Africa as elsewhere, had become a two-edged tool, condemned most vociferously by those victimised by it, extolled by those who used it, and tacitly recognised as useful under specific circumstances by those leaders and nations who could envisage a day when wars would be stamped out almost before they could be decently got underway, leaving them little else as an alternative to terrorism.

Certainly, in the forseeable future, terrorism will have a fresh reason for existing. Discernible through the current mists of confusion and lost faith is the scarred, broken, and gradually expiring body of Rising Expectations. The centuries-old belief that economic growth is continual, is dying. It may have been, as innumerable economists, social scientists and philosophers have believed unyieldingly that economic growth was indispensible to the security and orderly progress of humanity, but the clear fact appears quite evident that economic growth founded upon exploitation of unlimited natural resources, simply cannot survive the depletion of the world's resources. It is not just the fact, but also the philsophy.

Whatever may ensue from this, including an excellent probability that no aspect of human existence will escape alteration, it can reasonably be expected that change, which has never come peaceably, will not do so this time, either. Not the kind of change that has destroyed the fantasy of everlasting resource and economic self-sufficiency.

The bounty is gone. Existence based on plundering without replacing is moribund. Economic superstates such as Japan which have grown great as a result of voraciously consuming the produce of others, will change, and will decline. One morning everyone will arise as they always have, and go to the window — and the sun will be gone.

From this kind of change and all its inevitable upheavals arises every element essential for terrorism. All the counter-cultures, mindless and otherwise, which have been willing chaos, can be expected to exult in the new genesis. Every nihilist will discover in the wrenching change his reason, as well as his excuse, for destroying the good with the bad, among all the things he was never able to create.

The third way thrives in vacuums. It flourishes and fattens where change is resisted. It becomes strongest where dissent and confusion divide people. It not only spawns where demoralisation exists, it brings along its own, vaster demoralisation. It can no more be legislated out of existence than can crime. It may replace small wars, but it will just as likely create a situation where the big war takes precedence.

Terrorism in the 'sixties preoccupied the authorities of Europe and America as a phenomenon which left them baffled and groping. Terrorism in the 'seventies progressed beyond the stage of simple murder and vandalism, except in the regional and social spheres, to emerge as a third force, distinct from the traditional resources available to dissenters — insurgency, rebellion, civil disobedience. It began to be recognisable as something more substantial than racial or regional resistance. Terrorists, regardless of ideological affiliation, could meet anywhere on common ground. They could exchange information and intelligence. They could pool experience and expertise, share sanctuaries, actively support one another's counter-cultures without particularly believing in them or even understanding them.

By the 'seventies they had become outwardly and discernibly what they had been developing into for over a decade, inhabitants of the Fourth World, advocates of the third way, activist practitioners of a variety of nihilism specialising in all the methods and techniques developed to create confusion through violence and destruction.

Generally, they professed leftism. Many actually were leftists. Others favoured leftism because it provided the funds, arms, and most often the essential underground escape routes and sanctuaries. They served leftism, as in Uruguay, with genuine dedication; they made great sacrifices to help Uruguay's Tupamaros reach for control of the nation, but they were never serving the cause of dissent as much because they despised oligarchs and oligarchic democracy, as because they wanted Uruguay as a hemispheric base from which to function as destroyers of other countries, other economies, and other people.

As counter-culturists, terrorists have synthesised the majority opinion against counter-cultures, which is unfortunate. Most great social changes were the result of counter-cultures. Terrorism is — and is not — a counter-culture. It is, in the sense that it seeks to compel change, and it is not in that it does not advocate any kind of progressive change, instead it advocates chaos and lawlessness.

Japan's *Rengo Sekigun*, or Red Army, was not an ideological discipline based upon communism, as its leaders claimed. It was a purely nihilist organisation, which, could it have achieved control of Japan, would have set the hordes to marching, to destroying, to devastating.

Terrorists talk of 'new orders', but they simply do not create nor implement them, and their excuse for not doing so has been that there can be no order, no peace, no reconstruction, until all the world has been subjugated. Well, that is nihilism pure and simple, because all the world could never be subjugated, and they would therefore be killing, laying waste, looting and destroying for as long as it was possible for them to do so, without creating.

In the Middle East, in Asia, in Europe with far less success to-date at any rate, terrorism has out-grown its former image of spectacular vandalism and violence, which is not to say another massacre such as the one which occurred in Germany during the last Olympiad could not occur. Terrorism into the 'seventies faces greater opportunities to become a legitimised factor in both the chancellories and the ghettoes. The winds of change are blowing with increasing velocity. The elements of opposition to change are entrenching. A vacuum of vulnerability is spreading world-wide in the place of the expiring body of thought which has for two hundred years held that economic and resource exploitation could provide the only means for human progress.

Into this ready-made, widening and deepening vacuum, the forces of terrorism will most certainly infiltrate, but not as the vandals of the 'sixties, rather as the Huns and Tartars of the 'seventies, bringing as their alternative to a careful and prudent groping for the new values, their third way.

Index